AWAKENING

Robert Earl Burton (2016)

Awakening

Quotations from
Robert Earl Burton

*A conscious teacher explains
how to recognize higher states of awareness and
how our own Higher Centers may awaken.*

Collected and edited
by Dianne Crosby

FELLOWSHIP OF FRIENDS

2017

Awakening

Quotations from Robert Earl Burton
Collected and edited by Dianne Crosby

Published in 2017 by Fellowship of Friends Publishing
Post Office Box 1000, Oregon House, California 95962
publishing@beingpresent.org

FIRST EDITION
Library of Congress Control Number: 2017941409
ISBN: 978-0-692-75291-3

Front cover: "Swan in Flight" 2017 photo from Shutterstock.
Frontispiece: Robert Burton (2016) by Ann Douglass
page 167: Image of Phoenician goddess
© Marie-Lan Nguyen / Wikimedia Commons

This book is dedicated to our beloved teacher Robert Earl Burton and to all of his students – past, present, and future. He taught us to find our own Third Eye. Such luck! Such Presence.

Contents

Everyone appears in this life in a vessel that is asleep, but the vessel carries a Third Eye that can awaken. Our first quest is to bring Presence and our second is to make it permanent.

One eventually turns everything into Presence – Higher Centers consume sleep.

— *Robert Earl Burton*

Introduction

"How do you know if you are experiencing Higher Centers?"

This is a common query from those who have begun working with the ancient system of awakening taught by George Gurdjieff, Peter Ouspensky, and Robert Burton (hereafter called "the Teacher"). The system emphasizes Higher Centers as the seat of higher states of consciousness. If fully functioning Higher Centers, also known as Third Eye, are the goal, then how are they to be recognized? Good question.

As a student of the Teacher for thirty-seven years, I had asked this question myself and had seen it addressed many times, both in words and through non-verbal actions of the Teacher and others. It was raised once again at an Autumn 2013 meeting of the Teacher's students held in the mountains of upstate New York. Some of us at the meeting responded with insights and examples, but time only allowed for a few short responses. Afterwards, it occurred to me that much more could be brought to this subject – from the Teacher himself – if a selection of his teachings on this subject were gathered in one place. The result is this collection of direct quotations from the Teacher. It is the long response to the question about Higher Centers.

What follows in this Introduction is intended as background for those wanting a guide to the concepts underlying the Teacher's esoteric thought. The Teacher's personal work, grounded in the Gurdjieff-Ouspensky system, led him to his own experiences of Higher Centers. He began teaching in 1970 with the aim of helping each of his students discover his or her own Third Eye.

Emblazoned on the forehead of an artwork of an enlightened being, Third Eye symbolizes the human potential to connect with a higher reality through an awakened or higher state of awareness. These higher states are known by many names, including Higher Centers, Self-remembering, Presence, and the Higher Self. It is this elevated state that is the central subject of this book.

The system did not originate with the Teacher nor with Gurdjieff – they teach that it is ancient wisdom passed on from a wide variety of sources. Many of its ideas and methods remained relatively unknown in the West until the 20th century when individuals such as Gurdjieff, Ouspensky, and the Teacher began to write and teach others about awakening.

Whether this system is for you depends on your aim: If you want to make more money or become a better athlete, look elsewhere. But, if you want to understand the nature of reality, or you desire self-knowledge, or you wish to feel closer to God, or to serve others, the system can help. Anyone with such aims may benefit from experiencing higher states because more can be seen and understood in a higher state. It is as if the light bulb has gone on and a new comprehension of reality lives inside you, continuing to inform your actions long after the state has passed.

Virtually everyone has the potential for experiencing a higher state because its seeds exist in the human body from birth. Although Higher Centers are dormant in most adults, there are ways to encourage them to wake up and grow. Discovering them begins by learning to recognize your own inner child, which the system calls essence. It is the part of you that can be open to the moment, just like a child or a beginner; it is also the part that can learn to recognize when you are experiencing a higher state.

Essence includes physical and psychological traits as well as talents and weaknesses. More importantly, it includes a clear core of awareness that is the root of all higher states. In brief, the term essence refers both to a set of personal traits and a child-like state. While talents in essence should be developed, what is more important is finding the state of essence, which can then connect directly with Higher Centers.

For those interested in awakening the issue becomes a practical one: how to help essence transcend into the Higher Self. This requires cleansing yourself of useless self-absorbed thoughts and pretentious acts while training the attention, or mindfulness, that you bring to each moment. Whether the moment involves an object, a task, or another person, essence can learn to divide its attention between itself and that which it perceives. When you reside in a state of divided attention you are "Self-remembering." This does not mean multi-tasking. Quite the opposite – it means being fully engaged in an activity while doing it and being aware of yourself doing it at the same time.

As a form of attention, Self-remembering can be practiced anywhere, any time. By comparison, some traditions focus on the quality of attention only during particular activities, such as formal meditation; sometimes physical separation from ordinary life is also required. Self-remembering, however, is not restricted to a particular time, nor to a place such as a prayer rug or temple, nor does it require special clothing or objects such as icons, beads, or drugs. With Self-remembering, one can experience ultimate reality wherever one may be while attending to whatever is in the moment.

In sum, the system is for people who live ordinary lives with jobs, families, and other activities. It is based on balancing all parts of yourself, while maintaining an openness to transcending your ordinary capacities to experience new organs of perception: your Higher Centers. Central to this endeavor is learning to recognize the state of essence and making efforts to help it thrive in the present. When the Higher Self emerges in a state of Self-remembering, essence does not disappear – states are cumulative and, during a higher state, essence simply participates in the moment.

Recognizing Your Inner Child

One definition of Self-remembering is "essence aware of itself." Essence unaware of itself can be seen in infants. A newborn gradually becomes aware of its surroundings and directs its attention there, but the very young child is not aware of being a self nor of having awareness. The child does not perceive itself, thus it does not know itself.

If essence becomes simultaneously aware of both itself and what it perceives, then essence remembers itself. Although it is usually a wordless state, there is a strong sense of "me in this place, with that." A vivid memory is created and one has a firm experience of self. This is true whether the memory is pleasant or unpleasant. Pleasant memory is formed, for example, when Higher Centers appear while perceiving beauty, experiencing joy, or enjoying insight. Unpleasant experiences, such as those involving pain or danger, may also evoke higher states because the most real part of oneself must deal with those events. Higher states, regardless of type, are valued by the system as the ground from which the Higher Self may emerge and in which it can evolve.

Although memories are useful in learning to recognize higher states, the real aim is to learn to experience higher states in the present rather than dwelling on the past. To employ this idea in the present, try looking for the state of essence in yourself or others; it often has a light-hearted child-like feeling. There may also be a sense of smallness or "little me" experiencing whatever is occurring. It is the part of you that is simple and sincere; it does not try to impress others or fake it through a situation. Learning to recognize this state requires effort, but once found, it is relatively easy to find again.

Alternatively, try seeing the opposite of essence, that is, observe what in yourself is personality, such as learned behaviors, acts, and attitudes. It is not that essence is good and personality is bad; it is a matter of seeing what is more real. Much of learned behavior is civilizing, but it is from essence that the Higher Self emerges.

Environment is also important to finding essence – an environment that is unfriendly to your inner child evokes the hard protective shell of false personality, which is a mask that thinks it is real. True personality, in contrast, is a mask that knows it is a mask. It is necessary to protect essence while interacting with life. Essence and true personality are promoted by avoiding extreme behaviors, violent impressions, sarcasm, and teasing. Other efforts that strengthen essence include the transformation of negative emotions and the enjoyment of fine impressions, such as good quality art, music, books, and nature.

Recognizing the Path

The path to the Higher Self both *emerges* from the same place in each of us (essence) and *converges* at the level of desiring something better or higher for one's life. Between these two points the path usually becomes obscured in the jungle of Maya (illusion), which is the world of desires, fears, imagination, and identification with the many ordinary aspects of life. It is the realm of "the many 'I's" – the many insubstantial, changing, and imaginary things to which we become attached.

A major source of illusion is our own lower centers. Sometimes called "the machine" by teachers of the system, the lower centers are the intellectual, emotional, moving, instinctive, and sex centers. Observing them is important to understanding their functions, correcting wrong work of centers, and becoming balanced so that Higher Centers may manifest. An even more important reason to study them is that it reveals what is not the Higher Self. We all tend to say "I" to each impulse from a lower center, but in truth, these many 'I's are not unified. They are not the Higher Self or Real 'I'.

Another reason to engage in self-observation is to find those parts of oneself that can assist in recognizing and traveling the path. The most helpful is the highest part of the emotional center. The Teacher uses the common deck of playing cards as a handy method of describing the centers and their various subparts. The suit of hearts represents the emotional center, with the king of hearts symbolizing the most intelligent part of that center. The king of hearts is the home of one's refined emotions, such as reverence, aesthetic appreciation, valuation for truth, and inner strength.

Because this king most closely resembles and aspires to Higher Centers, it can make efforts to be present and to support higher states when they appear. When playing this role the king of hearts is called "the steward." Although the steward can try to be present, it is Higher Centers themselves that can actually be present. When Higher Centers are not awake, it is the steward (especially a subpart called the nine of hearts) that can recognize this and both apply what has been learned in a higher state and initiate practical techniques to awaken Higher Centers.

A real path of awakening always has two elements: discovering your true nature and mastering your lower self. The concepts of essence and Higher Self concern developing your true nature; mastering the lower self involves seeing it for what it is and strengthening the king of hearts so that it may begin to bring order into the chaos of the many 'I's. While both elements are necessary, it is ultimately more important to focus on becoming the Higher Self which has the greatest ability both to experience Presence and to master the lower self. The idea of a Higher Self experiencing Presence while mastering the animal energies of the lower self is often depicted in art, for example, Shiva dancing on a demon or Christ standing on a snake.

In order to locate and follow the path between your inner child and your Higher Self it is necessary to find a conscious teacher and a school of awakening. Nobody sees himself, or herself, objectively; outside help is essential to success. This book is composed of quotations from a conscious teacher and it contains many of his richest insights. However, you cannot succeed with only a book, not even this one. Personal help of the right type is critical, as are good luck and your own efforts. For information on contacting a school, see the last page of the Introduction.

Recognizing Your Higher Self

Your Higher Self is a higher state; thus recognizing it requires a basic understanding of the system's theory of states of consciousness. The theory is that humans experience different degrees of awareness ranging from deep sleep to full wakefulness and beyond. On this sliding scale one may be closer to, or farther from, any particular point on the range of possibilities. The system divides this vast range of states into four levels. The lowest, with the least awareness, is the first state; it is what is commonly called sleep. It occurs when we retire to bed for deep rest and is characterized by dreams that are usually seen to be illusions or distortions of the world as we experience it after arising. The second state is where we eat, talk, read, drive cars, and so on. These two lower states are the medium for the lower centers and the lower self. The second state is often characterized as "sleep" because, as seen from higher states, it is just as full of illusions and distortions as the first state. It is, in effect, Plato's cave of shadows.

The third and fourth states are associated with Higher Centers. In the third state, Higher Emotional Center functions in addition to the two lower states and there is a greater awareness of reality as it pertains to oneself. In the fourth state, Higher Mental Center functions in addition to the other three states and one's awareness is again greater, including the perception of universal laws underlying reality. Becoming one's Higher Self through experiencing the third and fourth states brings with it discriminating awareness, enhanced understanding, and the warmth of compassion, which enable one to be one's Higher Self and to work within ultimate reality. Significantly, in these higher states you do not lose contact with "the real world" (second state), rather it is seen from a new perspective; that is with proper scale and relativity.

The problem is that many people have trouble recognizing a higher state when it happens. Odd as it sounds, you can be in a higher state and not know it. The Teacher says:

> Higher Centers can be quite lucid and clear and sharp, and they can be progressing without one knowing it.

> We often do not know when we are experiencing the Third State until we realize it in retrospect. It is the machine that recalls higher states of consciousness, not the state itself.

> A curious aspect of our false personalities is that they consider the Third State an interruption. It is foolish to talk about what we are after, when what we are after has appeared. *One must learn to recognize when higher states have emerged within one.*

There are several advantages to recognizing a higher state while it is occurring: the likelihood of sustaining it increases, you can better use what you see in a higher state, and you are more likely to find your way there again. To assist in recognizing the states associated with Higher Centers, Chapter 2 covers twelve common attributes of such states. It is unlikely that all twelve will be apparent in any one experience, yet, over time, these attributes or traits recur and are verifiable. A subsequent section covers what Higher Centers "are not," including parts of us that may masquerade as higher states.

It is also helpful to understand some of the reasons for difficulty in recognizing higher states. Foremost is imagination about them – if a state fails to match one's imaginary picture of what it should be, it will not be valued. For example, if "radiant bliss" or "great wisdom" is expected, a higher state that occurs in a simple moment or at a time of suffering will be discounted. Because one did not recognize it and value it, efforts to remain there were not made; thus its insights may have been viewed as ordinary thoughts, which have a tendency to be obscured or discounted.

One particular form of imagination is expecting that all higher states will resemble exceptional Fourth State experiences that one may have read about or even experienced. The difference between the Third and Fourth States is equal to, or greater than, the difference between the first state and the second state. Forgetting this difference may lead to missing the Third State, which is often quite simple. It is always right here, right now – a clear awareness of yourself, sitting here, reading these words.

Another common misunderstanding is that Higher Centers will always be the same and that they are either "on or off," like a light switch. To the contrary, they vary greatly in feeling and contents; moreover, they are constantly changing. In fact, they grow. At first, Higher Centers are like babies, simply pure awareness peering out. Represented in art as putti (baby angels), their development parallels that of children in that they gradually grow up. In such art young girls symbolize a maturing Higher Emotional Center while young boys symbolize the same for Higher Mental Center.

Other reasons for difficulty in recognizing higher states include being so absorbed in what Higher Centers "are not" that one loses track of what they "are." This can result in a reluctance to drop the steward in order that the Master, one's Real 'I' may appear. There is also the lower self with its many tricks, including the ability to masquerade as the Higher Self. A thorough familiarity with the stratagems of the lower self is helpful. They are addressed in Chapter 6. Finally, it is important to recognize that Higher Centers, even when mature, are always learning. They must educate themselves and each time they manifest they increase their being.

Fortunately for us, the Teacher has traversed this path and has shared what he has learned on his journey. He tells us "I have no desire to hide my footsteps – on the contrary, I wish to freeze them in print to enable others to escape." This book is possible because he allows us to follow him in just this way. It is a collection of his statements most of which appeared in print during his forty-five years of teaching between 1970 and 2015.

The Teacher employs many names or terms for Higher Centers: *Third Eye, Real 'I', Divided Attention, the Self, the Soul, Higher Mental Center and Higher Emotional Center, the Third and Fourth States, World 6 and World 12, the Astral Body, Transcendental States, Self-remembering, Higher Self, God-Realization, Four Wordless Breaths, Divine Presence,* and *Presence.* Each capitalized name or term of this sort should be understood to equate with Higher Centers. (See *Note on the Text* for additional clarification.)

In the end the name used for Higher Centers is unimportant compared to actually being in a higher state and discovering its benefits. If you would like additional information on the ideas of the system, try Robert Burton's book,

Self-Remembering, or one of Peter Ouspensky's books such as *In Search of the Miraculous.* Another invaluable resource is direct contact with other students in a school of awakening. For further information or to meet a school, please contact The Fellowship of Friends, Inc. at +1 (530) 300-5322. Additional information about the Fellowship is available on pages 167-168.

Dianne Crosby
Washington, D.C.

Note on the Text

The following text, meaning all of Parts I through VI, consists entirely of quotations from the Teacher; only the organization and subject headings are the editor's and are the result of seeing how the material sorted itself into topics. The sources used in collecting quotations for this book include:

> *Apollo Forum*
> *Apollo Miracle*
> Daily Cards
> Daily Card Binder (1975-1991)
> *Mount Carmel Journal*
> Quotations Database of FOF
> *Renaissance Journal*
> *Self-Remembering* by Robert Earl Burton
> (published by Samuel Weiser, Inc., 1991)
> *Thoughts From The Teacher*
> *Via del Sol Journal*

Because the Teacher often repeats ideas with minor variations in wording, this collection is a representative selection of his statements on recognizing and awakening Higher Centers. A sincere effort has been made to remain true to the spirit of his message and to cover the broad scope of his teaching. Minor editing was employed for consistency and readability. Any use of italics for emphasis within the quotations is from the original text.

With respect to the many names that the Teacher uses for Higher Centers, he makes few distinctions among them, except that he indicates a slight difference between "created light" and "uncreated light." Created light is the result of using the sequence; uncreated light is a higher state experienced without using a sequence. Please refer to the Glossary and Chapters 14 and 15 for further explanation of the sequence and created light.

Occasionally the Teacher speaks of Third Eye or Real 'I' as a place, or as a being, separate from the four wordless breaths. Nevertheless, it is clear that he intends the Four Wordless Breaths to be understood as full consciousness:

> The first part of the sequence is relative consciousness
> and the Four Wordless Breaths are full consciousness.

Even so, he consistently ranks uncreated light a little higher than created light. Thus, when the term "four wordless breaths" occurs in the same sentence as another term for Higher Centers, four wordless breaths is not capitalized in deference to the other term. Also, when more than one term for Higher Centers is used in a sentence, in order to indicate emphasis or to enhance readability, not all terms are capitalized.

This clarifies the Teacher's terminology and the pattern of capitalization, but, more importantly, all of these names are merely symbols for a higher reality. Consciousness is not words; it is, generally, a wordless state. In addition, although a picture may be worth a thousand words, images too are merely symbols. Higher states are beyond names, language, and even the symbols, images, or metaphors used to represent them.

Acknowledgments

Many people have helped to make this collection of quotations available. Foremost, of course, is the Teacher himself. Under his direction his formal meetings were recorded, transcribed, and transformed into printed journals. Since 2007, an electronic database of quotations from his meetings has also been maintained.

The Teacher lives the work and encourages his students to be the words at all times, thus he also brings light to informal circumstances such as a casual meal or museum visit. Those with him in such circumstances are encouraged to take notes of what he says and these notes, too, are often used for written sources relied on for this book.

While many have assisted with the process of turning his spoken words into print over the past forty-five years, the Teacher generally reviewed and supervised the issuance of printed matter to his students. It is impossible to name all those who participated, but we are indebted to them for their efforts to capture and preserve the essence of this essentially oral teaching.

As this book took shape several individuals provided encouragement and assistance by evaluating and commenting on the material collected and by providing helpful suggestions. Those in this "inner circle of the book" include: Ilene and Richard Ackerman, William Bentley, Liza Casey, Helen Caton, Jeanne Chapman, Elizabeth Fraser, Liubov Hanson, Girard Haven, Greg Holman, Robert MacIsaac, Dorian Matei, Kimberly and Michael McDavit, Mary and Robert Moore, Peter Morrow, Bette Rintrona (who asked the question that sparked this whole endeavor), Michael Rolfer, William Scholte, Nicholas Spaulding, and Lindsey Van Wagenen.

Special thanks go to those who proofread and commented on the text once it was collected and organized. They were: Wilton Baker, Kevin Brown, Ruadhan Hayes, Paula Joudrey, and Susan Luccini.

More than special thanks go to my friend, advisor, and editor, Cynthia Schmidt, whose expertise guided this project with grace and insight.

Dianne Crosby
November, 2016

PART I
THE NATURE OF HIGHER CENTERS - THE HIGHER SELF

Higher Centers have a humble beginning. When one first experiences them, which may be for five seconds, a simple Presence without words is peering from one's machine.

The inexpressible luminosity of Divine Presence is who we are.

That which one truly possesses is without words and peers from one's forehead. It is one's infant Self.

Everything exists for Presence - for the sake of the conscious child within.

We are always two people: we are Presence, which is who we truly are - our Higher Self - and sometimes we become the lower self, which thinks it is God.

Who are you today? The lower self is many; the Higher Self is one and always the same.

Strive to be who you are - the Higher Self - and avoid being who you are not - the lower self.

CHAPTER 1

States of Consciousness

There are four states of consciousness that man is capable of experiencing. The first state is sleep; that is, when one retires in the evening and freshens accumulators. It is a vegetative, non-existent state. The second state of consciousness is called the "waking state." This state is characterized by the hypnotism of movement of one's machine which produces the illusion of reality. In this state one speaks, listens, reads, writes, and so forth. These two states are the natural condition of man. Associating the idea of consciousness with these states is misleading, as both are mechanical and in reality differ little from one another.

The Third and Fourth States ... *are not mechanical.* The Third and Fourth States are the natural medium for one's Self. One's Higher Centers are two beings, Higher Emotional and Higher Mental, and they form true unity. These two higher states cannot appear simultaneously and can be produced only with great effort. One verifies the existence of Higher Centers when one experiences a state of Presence silently peering from one's machine. When this occurs it is useful not to try to distinguish which of the two is present, because intellectual inquiry can interrupt higher states. Generally, one's Higher Emotional Center is present in times of joy, whereas one's Higher Mental Center is present in times of sorrow and danger; even so, each has an emotional and an intellectual life of its own.

3

Mr. Ouspensky said that there are four states of consciousness, the first two of which differ very little from one another. In fact, the first two are states of unconsciousness, in which Third Eye is buried behind the swamp of imagination. World 12 and World 6 are states of consciousness.

The second state is more under one's control than the first state.

The first state promotes the illusion that the second state is real.

Higher Centers are designed to serve humanity. Jesus said, *Whosoever will be great among you, shall be your servant.* When Higher Centers appear they begin with the first line of work, that is they begin for themselves. When people meet a school, they are expected to work almost exclusively on the first line of work, and later, when they can start thinking of others, they work on the second or third line. And the process commences again at a much higher level. When Higher Centers first appear, they exist for themselves and later they exist to serve others. In the East the machine is represented as a lamp. When it is rubbed a genie appears and grants three wishes, that is, he serves. If I were given three wishes, I have elected that they should be repetitive: *Thy will be done. Thy will be done. Thy will be done.*

Ouspensky was asked, "Why is the devil so powerful?" and he responded, "Because we do not know enough about him." In fact, you do not know enough about yourself, and if you do not know who you are, how can you know who you are not? Know thyself – know the Third and Fourth States of consciousness. *If you do not know those states, you cannot know when the king of clubs is pretending to be you.*

CHAPTER 2

Twelve Attributes of Higher Centers

1. SIMPLICITY

Essence turns into Higher Centers. A beautiful, childlike state becomes aware of itself and aware of what it observes.

It is absolutely necessary to sustain essence and to build on it in order to reach Presence.

What is Presence but essence aware of itself? A simple, gentle child.

Essence alone is insufficient – it must become aware of itself and so transcend itself in Presence.

Essence Presence is a timeless, ageless state – essence is the bridge to Higher Centers.

Self-remembering is a return to essence, only this time essence is aware of itself with consciousness.

Self-remembering is the art of raising the conscious child within you.

The higher one's state, the sweeter and simpler it is.

The Third Eye is genuinely simple, while the lower self is artificially complicated.

All of our exercises nurture essence: not expressing negative emotions, avoiding wit and teasing, controlling gesticulation.

A great deal of Self-remembering is recognizing the sublime within the common. Our lives comprise so many common moments, so many common miracles.

There is an art to every second. By being present to small things, one unites the smallest and the greatest.

Western art uses cherubs to represent essence Presence. Self-remembering, Divine Presence, is the eternal fountain of youth, eternally young.

Children are in a perpetual state of discovery, as are Higher Centers.

With Divine Presence, evolution becomes real and not merely symbolic of reality.

The child within becomes aware of itself – this is evolution.

2. PRESENCE

Essence must transform itself into Presence in order to realize itself.

The Third State is your true identity. Third State is none of the many 'I's; it is one's Soul.

You are a state – the state that remembers is *You*.

We must remember that Presence is real; You are real.

The Third Eye is who you are.

The most important person you will ever meet is your Self – you are that person.

The Third Eye is master of the invisible and the impossible; he alone can see the lower self; he alone can know himself.

To know thyself means to produce World 12, one's Higher Emotional Center.

For the Soul to know herself she must be herself – be present.

A large part of knowing one's Self is knowing what one is not.

It comes down to the desire to accept Presence or the lower self as one's Self. *There is nothing in between. It is either this state or imagination.*

In addition to knowing one's Self, one has to create one's Self and this is the labor of ages, of nine lifetimes.

Remember, that when your Astral Body is present, your Soul is a conscious stranger in an unconscious strange land – your physical body.

Student: Are we actually creating Souls by trying to remember ourselves? Precisely. That is the meaning of life on earth; everything else is biological. William Wordsworth wrote 'the child is father of the man.' With Self-remembering, the man is father of his child – Higher Centers.

The Third State is uncomfortable and also comforting. It is foreign to us.

Your Third Eye has been in a different body before.

Each of our lives is a temporary stepping stone on the way to eternal Presence.

Every lifetime brings a new name, but Presence is nameless.

You are playing the role of your name; each day a script is written especially for your evolution.

World 12 emerges when you divide attention.

Man can only live through the presence of the Higher Emotional Center, the living God.

God means "Presence in man."

Formatory mind thinks that dividing attention should be quite emotional, but in reality a state of Divided Attention encompasses a wide spectrum of emotions – the Soul has many hues.

Nothing is as exhilarating as Divine Presence. It is the one thing that is ours. It is the one thing that counts. It is the one thing that we can keep forever.

Consciousness has degrees. Presence can have more or less intensity.

Divided Attention is Self-remembering. They are synonymous.

Higher Centers are not what one would think they are. *They are!*

Nothing can be higher than recognizing and honoring Divine Presence within oneself. That is recognizing God within one's Self. There can be no mystical experience without Presence.

Self-remembering is the divinity within you.

The Presence of Higher Centers is a reward unto itself, as they exist in what Buddha called 'the eternal now.'

If you want to go to heaven, be present now.

Higher Centers are always quite close. All I have to do is hand a knife rest to the person next to me and, magically, they present their Self.

Presence gives mass to any situation. The situation may be absurd, but if you are present to it, Presence lends it mass.

The trick is to *BE* wherever you are.

One's Self is metaphysical, or other than physical, and yet it can shine forth lucidly for three minutes or three seconds. That is *You*. One needs to gather these little moments of consciousness when one can. If at the end of the day one has remembered one's

Self for one minute, it is not an occasion for disappointment, but for gratitude. After years of such effort, something real emerges.

3. MODESTY

Higher Centers are not impressive. It is more in the nature of the instinctive center to look impressive.

It is in the nature of awakening to be inconspicuous.

Be comfortable with inconspicuous Presence.

We are working at our highest level when we are in essence, content to be invisible and present.

Third Eye hides by being inconspicuously present. The lower self destroys itself and Higher Centers by being conspicuous rather than inconspicuous.

The lower self wants conspicuous changes; the Higher Self wishes inconspicuous Presence.

Life's idea of a conscious being is someone who is visibly awake – that does not exist.

The more conscious one becomes, the less one will occupy space.

When you are present the instinctive center is visible to you and invisible to others.

People without the answer want it to be big and conspicuous. Those who have it want it to be small and inconspicuous.

The sequence removes the lower self's desire to be conspicuous and leaves us with inconspicuous Divine Presence.

Self-remembering makes one softer and more gentle.

Never forget: simple inconspicuous Presence is all we are.

4. SILENCE

We do not have to say something – just *be* something. Higher Centers observe the world as it is: Presence without thought.

One of the most important things that one can learn is that the answer is not words, but a state.

Self-remembering is not a verbal process.

We find ourselves in silence and lose ourselves in unnecessary talk.

The Third State makes people quiet.

The nature of the Third State is quiet and still. It can also be quite electric and difficult to bear.

This silent state is who we are.

Most people are afraid of silence because they do not have this state of Presence to insert in place of the ten thousand 'I's.

The minimal nature of the sequence gives us an incredible hint: avoid words, choose wordless Presence.

Presence does not want to talk about itself; it wants to be itself.

Real 'I' is another name for Presence. Real 'I' is wordless. Schools avoid using the word "I", because the lower self is each 'I' that comes along. We rarely use the word 'I' because 'I' is not a word – it is this state.

One has to know for oneself what is Real 'I' because many deceitful 'I's call themselves Real 'I'.

We can speak about anything if we are present because we try to have Self-remembering moving behind speech.

If one speaks with Presence one will not speak unnecessarily.

Our meetings nourish our highest aspirations and teach us to be present throughout the week without words; speech plays but a small part in the realm of Cosmic Consciousness.

The story of our lives: speak a little less, speak a little softer.

The greatest secret is to be the words, not to talk about them.

5. CLARITY

Only Higher Centers can bring us the clarity of consciousness.

As one changes one's level of being, one increasingly sees the obvious. There is more of one to see it with.

The system is like a finger pointing the way to one's own Higher Centers.

The lower self receives identity from knowing esoteric ideas, while Higher Centers receive identity from understanding them. This is because the process of understanding brings Presence.

To understand the system is to be present.

The vision of my Higher Centers is a totally different experience than the vision of my body.

With Higher Centers functioning, it is like being able to see among blind men. It is truly that different.

The immortal vision of Third Eye transcends all mortal sight.

We are looking through our eyes – with Third Eye itself.

With Divine Presence, one has the gift of seeing oneself.

Consciousness reveals all things unaccompanied by Presence to be foolish.

True faith comes from the conscious vision of the Higher Emotional Center.

When one experiences Higher Centers, many questions are immediately answered, and one is able to discern what is real and what is not.

A diamond resembles Higher Centers more than any other stone, yet one must remember that this is only an analogy. Higher Centers are unlike anything on this level.

Diamonds symbolize Higher Centers because diamonds have no shadows.

The Higher Centers monitor the four lower centers and decide what to allow or disallow.

World 6 is the Master of the house; World 12 is the Mistress.

Student: What is it like to be conscious? Lighter than air, clearer than water, younger than springtime. The nature of Higher Centers is light and cheerful.

The present is not always beautiful, but it is always beautiful to be present.

When you are in your instinctive center it is like being in a dark room, but when you are present it is like a light bulb has gone on.

The first state is like dark night, the second state like fog, the Third and Fourth States like clear sunlight.

We are escaping from a dark place – the earth – and our little Higher Centers are little points of light, like stars.

As a school, we try to specialize in lighting fixtures because light represents Presence. Light consumes darkness.

Self-remembering is the light.

When you are remembering your Self you are in a state of relativity rather than of opposite thinking.

Higher Centers are quite wise and gentle.

Higher Centers see the transience of all things except Self-remembering; they see the young in the old and the old in the young, the end in the beginning and the beginning in the end.

Conscience is an emotional understanding of truth, generally in relation to behavior and to people.

Conscience comes from consciousness. Doing things that are good for your evolution helps conscience to grow.

Through Divine Presence we possess immortal wisdom.

There is absolutely no wisdom without Presence.

Never imagine wisdom to be more than the Presence of the conscious child within.

6. HUMILITY

Humility is an attribute of Presence, which is grateful simply to be. Humility is at the opposite end of the lower self, which is vain and ungrateful. Whatever is the opposite of the lower self is what we want – Consciousness.

Observe what resents or opposes humility and you will see why humiliating shocks are necessary. Additionally, humiliating experiences are given to one because they produce Higher Centers. Higher forces do not offer the gift of Consciousness to a machine that is other than mild and docile.

One is nothing without Self-remembering; so one must learn to be present, and through being present, one not only learns but also becomes what one is – one's Self. Our Higher Centers are naturally quite simple and humble and present.

Self-remembering must work with each simple moment because this is what comprises one's life. False personality may wait for large events and thoroughly fail.

Presence is content to recognize itself in the simplest object or impression such as a small, inconspicuous flower in the gutter.

No shock is too unimportant to create Presence.

Humiliation produces the Third State – one's humble Soul. One must experience humiliation often throughout one's life to create one's Astral Body.

To awaken one must be able to endure humiliation. No one has ever been exempt from this. One is given what one needs. There is no way to escape humiliation; it is almost a daily part of one's work.

What is humiliated within but false personality? True personality is not humiliated and neither is essence. If one feels humiliated, one is identified.

Humility with Presence displaces features.

Try to stay small. The lower self has an inflated imaginary picture of itself. Whether conscious or unconscious, we are all quite small.

Third Eye is content to be small and inconspicuous.

We are only special when we realize that we are not special. We are blessed with inconspicuous humility and Presence; it is this that makes us special. With Presence, everything leads to humility.

7. UNITY

Flashes of Higher Centers can become unified, that is, they can become a permanent state. They are one's true identity, the other you are, your Soul, *You.* This is the dimension of your existence which can pass from one vessel to another.

Higher Centers are unified, that is, they are the state of unity.

The greater part of unifying one's thinking is to ignore most of the 'I's. The many 'I's are not one, but what observes them is one. You are what observes – Real 'I'.

Our Higher Centers are conscious harmony and are like children – Hansel and Gretel. Do not concern yourself which one is present. Just be grateful that one of them is present.

Higher Centers are both male and female – World 6 and World 12. They are not sexless, however; they are Tarot Card XXI – "the

Peaceful One, powerful radiance." They are not the steward or the nine of hearts. There is no competition between Worlds 6 and 12, however, Higher Emotional Center does most of the work. Unbelievable, graceful external consideration exists between them.

As one works with emotions, channeling them with the sequence towards Presence, what is largely developed is the Higher Emotional Center. As World 12 develops, World 6 emerges from it.

Male and female humans are intended replicas of Higher Mental and Higher Emotional Centers.

Unity is a property of a man number five, so a part of your evolution is to observe yourself disintegrating into different personalities at various times, some of them much less favorable than others. It would be naive to expect a man number four to be the same person in every circumstance.

Only when you are becoming unified can you see that you are not unified.

Nothing should be higher than the Soul. This is why it is so regrettable when the lower consumes the higher and takes the place of one's Self. Such is the lamentable nature of not being unified.

When one identifies with the many 'I's, one ceases to be unified; when one separates from them, one becomes more unified.

We are living in a fairy tale with Divine Presence. Everyone is his own prince and princess – Higher Mental and Higher Emotional Centers, World 6 and World 12.

Awakening, as our school experiences it, is a very inconspicuous and meek process, producing the two gentle and sweet Higher Centers – Hansel and Gretel – conscious children.

8. LOVE

Higher Centers are love, will, and consciousness.

Love is a real characteristic of the Higher Self, whereas hate is an attribute of the lower self.

What is love? The Divine Presence of one's own Higher Centers.

There is an enormous amount of love hidden in essence, and, if we do not express negative emotions, then conscious love is allowed to flower.

The language of Higher Centers is divine, silent love.

I do not speak any foreign languages, but the language of Higher Centers I understand quite well.

When you are present you are a conscious being capable of conscious love.

The only way to express love is through consciousness.

Love must not merely be a word, but a state.

Finally, we are without words, and we are. Love emerges as the highest understanding.

Love – Influence C – hath touched and held all of us. Conscious love is the only real love on the earth.

It is a law that Influence C love us more than we love them. Never doubt they love you, even if they are turning you upside down.

Conscious love is the speech of the gods.

The way to escape is to take your own Presence as the Beloved, rather than someone external. However, when we look at each other with Presence, we have an external Beloved as well.

Presence is strongest when we are together – always.

Spending time with students speeds up your evolution.

For the Third Eye, the best impression is a fellow ascending Soul being present.

The more conscious one is, the less instinctive one is, and the more love one has.

Let us toast to the development of our Higher Centers. "Blossom of love, may you bloom and grow, bloom and grow, forever."

9. WILL

There can be no true will without Higher Centers being present.

Will is Self-remembering, and being present is will-power.

The lower self is willful – the Higher Self is conscious will.

Will is developed by overcoming weaknesses, which is why weaknesses are knitted into the machine.

We try to stay as far away from the lower self as possible, which produces its opposite – the Higher Self and Presence. Whatever stands between you and your Self, let it go.

As one's Higher Centers develop, one finds separating from the 'I's more interesting than listening to them.

If one sincerely tries to separate from the 'I's, one will succeed. Otherwise, one falls prey to the ten thousand.

Whatever you separate from produces *You*.

Ultimately, one must release everything but one's Self.

Happily, verification of sleep briefly produces Higher Centers. One of the best ways to remember one's Self is to separate immediately from the disappointment of realizing one has been asleep.

You really must relinquish negative emotions for your work to be successful. You really must want to release them and let

Third Eye appear. Your Soul is the pearl of great price and, like any pearl, must be created by transforming irritation.

Intellectual parts of centers try to keep one near the Third State of consciousness. Even so, the word "will" is a word, whereas the experience itself is a non-verbal state.

We are fortunate that there is a way out and that we can use higher parts of centers to reach Higher Centers.

Separating from injustice can produce Higher Centers.

Receiving friction where one expects support provides an extraordinary opportunity for transformation.

There is nothing more mechanical than expressing negative emotions, and nothing more conscious than transforming them.

Whenever one transforms negativity one gains time, the time of Higher Centers which are immortal. When one is negative, time has been lost to false personality.

The major barriers to the transformation of negative emotions are resentment and self-pity.

We often reach Self-remembering by quickly transforming self-pity.

It is the Higher Centers that transform suffering into consciousness. The machine wants a Disneyland version of awakening – no suffering. It is not possible.

Through the transformation of suffering one passes through dark periods and produces conscious light, one's Self.

Transforming suffering will always be the way out – not suppressing it, but transforming it into Presence.

Suffering is transformed through non-identification.

Gratitude towards friction is transformation of suffering.

Suffering is not transforming suffering.

When you transform suffering you become at least neutral and, when it has subsided, grateful.

One cannot transform imaginary suffering into Self-remembering; one can transform only real suffering into higher states. Except to form a magnetic center, suffering is not of value.

Christ and Socrates personify the ultimate transformation of suffering among conscious beings; the former was called upon exceedingly young to his trial, the latter, exceedingly late.

Difficult mechanical groups of 'I's that reappear enable our own conscious Higher Centers to reappear when they transform the 'I's into Divine Presence.

I would have no will without Influence C. There can be no conscious will unassociated with the will of the gods. Anything else would be incorrect crystallization.

One is most awake when transforming suffering and most asleep when complaining about suffering.

10. ACCEPTANCE

One can remember one's Self more if one does not wish the moment to be other than it is, and accepts it as it is.

One's Self is a neutral state which is not subject to the extreme sways of duality. A neutral state is not a vegetative condition, rather it is a state of nonattachment which combats imagination; it is a state of remembering one's Self.

When the Third State makes its appearance, accept it. There is nothing finer that you can accept than your Self.

It is not easy for men number four and five to accept Higher Centers when they appear, because their machines try to undermine Higher Centers when they appear through fear, indifference, or a variety of deceptions.

Always accept Presence on its own divine terms.

Nothing is insignificant for the Higher Self. The lower self calls mundane situations insignificant in order to devalue the importance of the moment.

No words are as touching as silence in the face of suffering. Even in the face of terminal illness, one still has the choice of being present and adding to one's Astral Body. One's time is counted, and time is nearly all that one has. There must always be friction of sufficient magnitude to produce consciousness.

Enduring friction without identification constitutes the greater part of our awakening.

Existence is simple. We have two centers that accept this and five that reject it.

It is one's attitude towards events, and not events themselves, which determines whether or not one will suffer.

When you enter the way, you are overloaded with responsibilities. Accept it when you are under pressure. If you accept, you are present. Grace under fire.

Some thrive on pressure; others wilt; only pressure can draw forth one's latent Higher Centers.

A major part of awakening is accepting one's conscious fate and life's unconscious fate.

Please have the aim to transform life's identification of the day, whether it is an earthquake or a riot.

It is important to take Influence C on their terms. Whatever they give you, try to bear it evenly.

We accept our task as given to us by Influence C.

By accepting, we transform suffering.

It is good to be accepting of friction. Everything we receive is necessary for our evolution or it would not be given.

11. SERVICE

Higher Centers are designed to serve humanity.

Conscious beings are for all times and all cultures.

When Higher Centers first appear, they exist for themselves and later they exist to serve others.

The more one advances, the less one is interested in taking awakening personally. One wishes to serve as one's valuation for this remarkable system increases. Features generally displace being of service.

One cannot develop immortal states that are selfish because they would be a curse in the universe rather than a blessing. For Higher Centers to come into being one must have the strength of external consideration.

In order to produce Higher Centers, one must learn the art of external consideration – a compassionate state accustomed to thinking about others.

The machine is self-serving whereas Higher Centers are servants and are externally considerate.

Higher Centers cannot be present if one is heedless of others. External consideration is practical and humane. Look for it in the small, as well as the great.

The essence of Self-remembering is self-forgetting.

Higher Centers can come to you when you are not thinking or talking about yourself.

Bringing out the best in others brings out the best in one's Self.

Do not support weaknesses in yourself or your friends; what is unconscious in us seeks what is unconscious in others. What is conscious seeks what is conscious in others.

Being present is the issue; you cannot help anyone unless you help your Self.

It is a waste of time to seek power over people and a sublime use of time to deliver people to their Souls through Self-remembering and transforming suffering. The instinctive center craves for power over people; the Higher Centers are nothing like that – they want to help people be present.

Eventually all of us will be so awake that we will be able to awaken someone else; the ability to externally consider will become that strong.

Student: If I became conscious, I would be isolated and live apart from society. This is why you are not conscious; your life would be all take and no give.

The Higher Self gives; the lower self takes.

Plato said, "The essence of knowledge is self-knowledge," and the essence of self-knowledge is Self-remembering, and the essence of Self-remembering is selflessness, and the essence of selflessness is to serve the gods consciously.

The system works if you use it, but it can also serve as a source of imaginary support unless one goes *beyond* it. *It is not sufficient simply to know one's machine, one must do something with it which ennobles oneself and humanity.*

We are most like God when we are externally considerate and selfless.

12. ETERNITY

Mental efforts can reach the level of Higher Centers, which escape time and death.

Certainly time is counted, but time is defeated with Presence. Someday this state will be all that is left.

If there is no Presence before death, there is no Presence after death.

Essence Presence crystallized becomes eternal. It is just us – our Higher Centers – nothing else – no other 'I's.

I know that time does not exist for Higher Centers – the word "immortality" means just that.

When we finally lay down our physical body, our Higher Emotional Center – World 12 – and Higher Mental Center – World 6 – are what survive.

When Higher Centers are present, everything else is brief and mortal.

Every second you remember your Self you pierce eternity.

World 6 and World 12 are the starry worlds in the microcosmic man ... they are considerably rarer than galaxies or stars.

Nothing in the universe can compare with Divine Presence in the microcosmos man or woman.

When one has a Third or Fourth State experience, it continues to resound throughout one's entire life.

Moments in which one experiences Higher Centers are imperishable. Try to understand the magnitude of this idea – it means one can be immortal because there is no ending for an ascending Soul.

Presence is immortality now.

Presence is simultaneously instant and infinite.

To grasp the infinite, one must become the infinite.

Higher Centers survive death, and lower centers do not. We live as if life will go on forever; it will not for the body, but it will for Presence. All things are impermanent except one's Self.

Swift is the passage of time and the end comes alarmingly fast. Nothing is more urgent than Presence.

AWAKENING

Courage Goodness,
and remember yesterday is gone
as tomorrow will be.
And in the end,
when death plays its despicable finale
upon this mortal flesh,
All that will be left
of each of thy laboring days
is thy Self.

(by Robert Earl Burton,
Via del Sol Journal, July 17, 1973)

PART II

THE NATURE OF THE BEAST –
THE LOWER SELF

Within man dwell together the Divine and the bestial. Beauty and the beast – Third Eye and the lower self.

The lower self is animal intelligence in human form and Divine Presence is angelic intelligence in human form.

Virgil said, "In every good man dwells nameless, dimly seen, a god." He is speaking about Higher Centers. They are often dimly seen, and we have to find a way to bring them to the forefront, to make them definite, to improve our focus.

It is either You, Presence, or it, the lower self. Either Presence becomes stronger or the lower self becomes stronger.

The machine cannot be present; Higher Centers within the machine, however, can be.

In order to observe one's machine, one must be remembering one's Self. For you see, my friends, it comes to this: if one is not observing one's machine, one is the machine.

Time spent outside the presence of Higher Centers must be seen as time wasted.

CHAPTER 3

Mired in the Many 'I's

Self-remembering is not mind activity; it is not the many 'I's.

There is no substitute for Third Eye, certainly not the ten thousand.

The many 'I's – the many lies.

We have to watch for our own 'I's terrorizing our Higher Centers.

The many 'I's wish to govern one's life, and only Self-remembering can displace them.

The many 'I's all come through the same speaker which creates the illusion that they are all one – the illusion of 'I'.

If you do not focus on the Third Eye, the only option left is the ten thousand. The many 'I's are false and fleeting, changing every three seconds, while the Third Eye remains constant and true.

Presence alone is sanity. The ten thousand are a madhouse.

The state of Presence is very reluctant to say the word "I," whereas the lower self uses it frequently. Often, when you say "I," you become "it."

When you are present, the many 'I's are paper tigers; when you identify with them, however, they are tigers.

If one experiences vicious, negative 'I's, one must not take them personally, nor feel guilty about having them. Our work is to transform them into Presence and, from that point of view, the worse the many 'I's are, the better.

If one forgives the ten thousand, one transforms them. If one keeps accounts, then they have an undetected victory.

The purpose of the lower self is to produce, through transformation, the opposite of itself – Divine Presence.

Third Eye is the pearl, and the lower self is the irritant that helps the pearl come into being.

There is always a way out. Whatever the many 'I's say, just "*Drop*" and "*Be.*"

The struggle with the many 'I's is not an endless battle. One eventually becomes fully conscious and escapes.

CHAPTER 4

Veiled by Imagination

The greatest sin in the universe is when the lower self masks Third Eye. The lower self is imagination. The Higher Self is consciousness. Being in imagination costs a human being his life.

Higher Centers find imagination extremely distasteful because it displaces them.

Sleep is the unconscious prevalence of imagination. Imagination is an addictive sleeping pill.

The easiest thing in the world is to be in imagination. There is nothing easier than to enter imagination and to stay there.

Higher Centers cannot come into being when one is immersed in imaginary problems. If one can abandon this shallow tendency in one's being, Higher Centers can be realized.

Higher Centers can only come if one stops thinking about oneself. Catering to the many likes and dislikes in one's machine is referred to in Zen as over self-indulgence.

Higher Centers will not manifest if one is self-indulgent.

Imagination satisfies all of the lower centers, but it does not satisfy Higher Centers at all.

It is critical to recognize the difference between Presence and imagination.

To escape, first you need to know that you are in prison. You cannot become twice-born if you do not know you are in imagination.

Although the lower self is incapable of recognizing something higher than itself, it is capable of destroying anything higher than itself.

When you do not see the lower self, he sees you and veils you.

We escape by chipping away little by little at what veils us.

What I am telling you is how I escaped sleep: I escaped by chipping away little by little at what veiled me.

We must not be fond of what veils us.

Technology is useful if one is present to it. It becomes a trap if one falls asleep to it, because one is fond of what veils one.

Marijuana sustains imagination and veils Third Eye.

Discovering who one is not is one of the best ways to know who one is. Presence is not a negative emotion. It is not indignant, nor impatient. It is humble; it is not pretentious. It does not think of itself as an important person, but as a person who is present.

Formatory mind and the queens crush Third Eye. The queens try to draw us closer to the veil. The queens try to draw us into stagnant prolonged imagination.

Try to be who you really are, and not who you think you are.

One needs to give up who one imagines one is to become who one truly is without imagination.

The lower self feeds on excess, the Higher Self on moderation.

The lower self offers imagination – plastic flowers – rather than Presence – real flowers.

Establishing Presence over imagination is the most difficult of all endeavors.

Fame usually takes the place of Presence for people. Life craves attention; schools, Divided Attention.

It is a great mistake to equate fame with consciousness.

The gods cannot reach men who suffer from an imaginary sense of self-importance.

If you talk too much, you cannot absorb; you superficially deflect rather than profoundly absorb.

When one laughs, the lower self seizes the current of sex energy that is intended to fuel Higher Centers and directs it towards itself. Higher Centers cannot appear while this is occurring.

The lower self depends quite a bit on humor and unnecessary talk to displace Presence.

In truth, one's laughter and one's Soul rarely commingle, for it is incredibly difficult to pierce imagination and remember one's Self.

Confusion and haste are very important ways for the lower self to displace Presence.

When you are confused, try to apply common sense to your actions: listen to the music, read the book, work – with Divided Attention – on the task at hand.

There is never any hurry when one is present.

Student: I find myself more and more in imagination. That is because your Self is appearing more and more frequently; it is a good sign.

Student: Is there one main obstacle to Self-remembering? Yes, imagination, which is the natural state of man.

Influence C have alerted us to our own condition and we have traded imagination for Presence. Only Influence C can lift the veil of imagination.

The gods are refuse collectors: they remove identification, imagination, and negative emotions. One sacrifices nothing but rubbish to awaken.

Try to find the principal subject of imagination as the lower self will use it repeatedly.

Often the way we defeat the lower self is just by ignoring him, not listening to his tempting 'I's.

One crushes the lower self by ignoring it.

How does one control the lower self? By focusing on the Higher Self. They happen simultaneously.

CHAPTER 5

Identified with Mechanical Functions

Our Higher Centers are not our lower functions. Surprisingly, they make their way because they are real and the lower centers are not.

The seed of genius is in the functions; Higher Centers' talent resides in inconspicuous Presence.

Talent and genius are given; Presence must be earned.

Higher Centers are simple and open. The lower centers are artificially complex and pre-occupied.

The machine's cunning way of remaining on the level of the functions is to engage in too many activities simultaneously. This leaves no room for Divided Attention.

We do one thing at a time with Presence. We choose the presence of Third Eye.

When you are present in the Third State, many parts of the machine that would be there in the second state disappear.

From one angle, the Third State has nothing to do with the four lower centers.

The Higher Centers must do what the lower centers try to do.

Third Eye is above all functions.

1. INTELLECTUAL CENTER

Higher Centers observe the world as it is, without thought patterns.

Knowledge cannot be a substitute for Self-remembering.

All schools in all ages had to transcend thought and arrive at wordless Presence.

Some people are satisfied with searching for esoteric knowledge, but not esoteric being.

Men number four must limit the time they think about ideas, because Self-remembering readily disappears behind words.

The lower self is satisfied with ideas, the Higher Self with reality.

The lower self tries to seize esoteric information and make itself the great interpreter.

The lower self wants to teach; Higher Centers are very grateful to be taught.

For us, real thinking would issue from the steward and the intellectual parts of centers. Higher Centers would discriminate what is of value or not. Each thought is an 'I' and the Soul is what observes these 'I's.

Formatory mind is strong in us. When we are actually in the Third State, the machine will look forward to describing that state.

When one is present, one must not think about the lower self. That is one of his tricks to lure you away from this state. He starts saying bad things about himself in order to draw you away from Presence.

It is painful for the lower self to agree; it would much rather argue.

When one argues, even if one is right, one is wrong.

The lower self wants to be right, whereas Presence wants to get it right.

The higher right is that which makes us present.

Consciousness is a state, not an opinion.

Intellectual expression is not the Self.

People either forget, or do not understand, that words are only symbols that point to a silent reality.

With regard to unnecessary talk, everything one does not say is a chance to be present, and everything one says is a chance to lose Presence.

Understanding that you are speaking is more important than someone understanding what you are saying.

Self-remembering is always the ultimate subject to grip.

Do not allow any subject to displace Self-remembering. It is far and away the most important subject one can occupy oneself with – to be or not to be present.

The more one speaks, the less possibility one has of actualizing what one is speaking of, because speech has a tendency to displace reality.

We must speak less about Presence and become silentlypresent.

2. EMOTIONAL CENTER

The system can only be understood – and withstood – from the king of hearts and Higher Centers.

When we focus on Presence we prevail over all illusions: age, sex, religion, color, nationality, health, home, parents, spouse, wealth, poverty, education, art, food, athletics, catastrophes.

It is difficult to give up one's imaginary picture of oneself because it is the ultimate vanity. However, if one does give it up, one becomes everything.

Often when people speak, it is from the tendency of essence to spill itself out, without having anything particularly useful to say.

To release negative emotions and let Third Eye appear, you must really want to. More than the subject, you must learn to control the source of negative emotions: the negative half of the queen of hearts.

The most incredible question never asked me is: "When do you see students most asleep?" They are most asleep when they are speaking about themselves.

The desire to be something or someone externally often inhibits the desire to be something internally.

Tragic occurrences in life can produce the Third State, but one has to be above feminine dominance in order to use them and not enter self-pity.

Feminine dominance means you are under the subjective sway of your own emotional center.

People travel everywhere but the present and try to save everything but themselves.

The principal way one can assist others is by remembering one's Self.

When one experiences contradictory emotions, it obliges one to drop the whole spectrum of the emotional center and stay with the present.

To gain conscious freedom we must control our emotional center and direct our attention to Higher Emotional Center – the divine presence of Third Eye.

Most all humans are subject to feminine dominance as they

were umbilically tied to their mothers at birth. If a person reaches Higher Centers he has given birth to his own child. This is the only true birth on this plane of organic life on earth.

3. MOVING CENTER

The lower self wants to move, but the Third Eye wants to stay right here.

When the moving center becomes too active, Third Eye disappears behind the veil of imagination.

Most people use their moving center to strengthen sleep; only in schools do people learn how to use it for Presence.

Sit down and stand up with Presence. That way, the master game is always on, not off and on.

Gesticulation creates the illusion of life. Outer quietness is preparation for inner quietness. Outer control of the moving center is preparation for inner control of the many 'I's.

Smoking and unnecessary eating and drinking keep the lower centers engaged and shut off Higher Centers.

Driving more slowly is a good way to remove the instinctive center from the driving experience. When one drives too fast, it is the lower self that is driving, thus bypassing Presence, promoting the illusion that the answer can be found outside of one's Self.

A lot of mechanical efficiency looks virtuous, but it is, in fact, treacherous.

Never sacrifice Presence for mechanical efficiency.

Nothing one does has any value unaccompanied by Presence.

4. INSTINCTIVE CENTER

The instinctive center thinks it is the center of the universe.

You are your Higher Centers, not your instinctive center.

Divine Presence is not an instinctive sensation; it is an inconspicuous reality. The instinctive center's idea of consciousness is something tangible, perceived by the senses, because that is all it has.

The instinctive center is a ruthless brain, and there is nothing it would not do to destroy the Higher Centers.

Perhaps the most important thing I could say about the instinctive center is that a great part of its deceit lies in convincing one that it is unintelligent, so that one will underestimate it.

You have to learn not to be fooled by your machine and the ways it tries to undermine your work.

Self-remembering must function even when the machine malfunctions.

A large problem of the lower self is that it tries to perform the inner meaning of the Holy Scriptures from the instinctive center only and will not step aside to let the Higher Centers enact the inner meaning.

The work is not something one does externally – it is internal. It is Third Eye engaging Divine Presence.

Student: I heard that you do not work with body types anymore. I still work with body types but, of course, consciousness is independent of type. The reason for knowing body types is to lead you to who you are. We want to be Third Eye, not our body type. Although people who meet the system are of different types, each has the potential to develop Higher Centers.

Only Presence can give value to our lives. Otherwise we are only machines surrounded by many other machines just like our own. There is a black, white, yellow, and brown version of every type. There are also male and female versions.

Student: What is the single best thing for awakening? Being present while eating, because if one can control the lower self while eating, one can control it in all other areas.

Try not to bury your Third Eye in the plate.

Desserts can bring essence without Presence.

Try to be present, especially in uninteresting circumstances. The king of clubs tries to occupy space passively through boredom and actively through the expression of negativity.

Undue alarm gives the machine a sense of reality at the expense of the Soul.

The lower self is the king of clubs – it opposes awakening because it thinks it is you.

The king of clubs is not capable of producing anything higher than itself, unlike the steward, which can produce Higher Centers.

Higher Centers wish to return to Presence, and the king of clubs wishes to return to imagination.

The king of clubs will use any card to pull one down from the Third State to the second state.

Even seemingly unimportant, mild 'I's are deadly and are used by the king of clubs to displace Presence.

The parts of centers are naïve to the fact that they are being used by the king of clubs to displace Presence.

Essence has limitations. It can be naive to the problem of the lower self, and thereby be used by it.

The lower self likes to be alone because it knows that other students may see it – its chances are best when we are by ourselves. The lower self does not want you to reach the Third Eye, and tries to isolate you as often as it can.

The notion of self is what seven billion people have. They have a notion of who they are, but, in fact, they are their lower self.

When the unconscious notion of lower self goes, Third Eye itself – God – enters.

5. SEX CENTER

The sex center is the highest order of mechanicality for organic life on earth. Just as the sun symbolizes World 12 on a mechanical level in the solar system, so our sex center represents World 12 in the human microcosmos.

Higher Centers, essence, and true personality require the energy of the sex center as do negative emotions, imagination, and identification. Thus our lives are composed of a struggle to direct the energies of our sex center to the former instead of the latter. Nature has endowed us with abundant sex energy, which can be used for physical union, transmutation, or both.

Man can create a god within by transforming the mystical energies of the sex center.

On one level the sex center is designed to perpetuate the species; on a higher level, it is intended to ignite the pineal gland[1], the seat of the Soul, through transmuting sex energy. Nature has endowed man with an enormous amount of sex energy, and we witness a similar design in nature when a huge amount of seed is cast from a single tree; each of those seeds could become a tree,

---

1. The pineal gland is a traditional symbol for the location of Higher Centers. However, the symbol probably should not be taken literally. One woman whose pineal gland was removed during brain surgery reports that she has no difficulty in experiencing higher states. Higher Centers seem to her to operate from a center located in that general area, even without a pineal gland.

yet few do. Generally, the sex center can only be photographed from Higher Centers, and even then it is a difficult process due to the elusiveness of that brain.

Student: How can we use sex energy profitably to establish reins to Higher Centers? Primarily through the non-expression of negative emotions, transmuting the mystical energies of the sex center. Without this process, one's essence and Higher Centers cannot emerge.

When one is not present, sex energy is being consumed in imagination. Imagination is a waste of time – a waste of sex energy. The body and the Higher Centers share the same supply of energy. This becomes more evident the older one becomes.

The lower self debases sex energy to a coarser level, turning it into imagination.

When we transform suffering we utilize sex energy to produce our immortal Astral Body.

Sex energy is a magical substance that can produce conscious children: Worlds 12 and 6.

It is quite simple: When one is present, sex energy enters directly into Higher Centers; during the sequence, it arrives there through the heart.

Through the sequence, sex energy is used by the heart to create Presence. This is inner creation.

Sex energy is used to produce an outer child and an inner child, but almost no one uses it for internal creation. For the instinctive center, immortality means physical procreation. In schools, it means creating the immortal conscious child within.

CHAPTER 6

Disguised as Higher Centers or "The Work"

Time is required for one to recognize a true higher state – as time passes, one will not so frequently be misled by certain parts of one that masquerade as Higher Centers.

People mistake nine of hearts activity or king of clubs activity for the presence of the Third Eye.

To rid himself of imagination posing as Presence is the great task of an ascending Soul in any school.

Every ascending Soul in every age must work with the same 'I's. What matters is not listening to them.

One's Self is like quiet water that is aware of itself.

If that which is observing is aware, both of itself and of the object viewed, Higher Centers are functioning. If a certain sternness accompanies that energy, however, one's instinctive center is most apt to be feigning Higher Centers. Each person must experience the process in which a lower function assumes the properties of consciousness.

The machine readily forgets that it is a machine; it is anxious to take itself for Higher Centers.

Each center has its own idea of consciousness and each takes itself as consciousness.

The machine cannot be present so it often attempts to undermine Self-remembering; almost all of the 'I's are a substitute for Real 'I'.

Among the many 'I's, which ones can you trust? None.

The lower self tries to look like the Higher Self.

The lower self is not what it imagines itself to be – it is an imitation of reality. The lower self does everything it can to imitate the state we are in now, but it is not this state.

The lower self likes to look virtuous while destroying the virtues …Egypt called it "Isis in her evil-coming."

The lower self is looking for esoteric secrets, while our little essence and Higher Centers have found them.

The machine can manipulate work 'I's causing one to analyze rather than to experience the present. Self-remembering is a very lean experience.

We must not stay at the level of the king of hearts, which can become an obstacle in itself. We want more than the presence of our king of hearts.

The Higher Self is quite content just to be itself.

Remember that the king of hearts is designed to fail eventually so that one's Higher Centers can emerge.

The nine of hearts is not the answer. Presence – Third Eye – is the answer.

Emotional ecstasy is highly prized in life, but the Higher Emotional Center silently controlling it is far superior.

When I entered St. Peter's for the first time, all of a sudden I began to experience a king-of-hearts crescendo. Third Eye immediately realized that I should freeze this response and receive the impression quietly with the divided attention of Third Eye rather than the ecstatic king of hearts.

The king of clubs wants to be Higher Centers, which it is not. When it tries to feign Higher Centers, it is emotionless – it has no charm.

Instinctive presence feigns individuality. Essence Presence is real individuality.

The lower self is heavy and gross and thinks it is light and beautiful. Even when it tries to feign Presence, it remains heavy.... Although he can pretend to be this state, he cannot actually be it.

There is a prejudice against consciousness being childlike. Because most men do not experience this state, they imagine Divine Presence to be hard and instinctive.

The sweetness and simplicity of essence is not taken seriously by the lower self.

The king of clubs can offer very poetic 'I's when Presence appears, in order to draw your attention away from the present.

The king of clubs would like us to believe that we have mastered it.

We must not lose time being appalled by the king of clubs, for that is part of its strategy.

You must not spend any time trying to reform your king of clubs.

The lower self is incapable of correction. One can control it, and one must keep it under control.

The lower self, in so many different ways, always says, "Look at me," rather than looking at God within.

It is a tragedy that the lower self draws attention to itself as that reinforces false personality and diminishes essence.

Subjective methods of awakening are rooted in the instinctive center and are, in reality, that center's way of expressing itself.

The lower self likes to think that he is better than others, which makes him worse. Vanity elevates itself above others and immediately becomes lesser. It is lower self-treachery.

One's center of gravity wishes to be one's Higher Centers.

Mechanical brightness is actually a curse if one cannot subordinate it to Divine Presence.

In *The Emperor and the Nightingale*, Hans Christian Andersen illustrated the tendency of mechanical parts of centers to pose as Higher Centers by having the Emperor substitute a mechanical songbird for the nightingale.

Chief feature is most anxious to classify its manifestations as favorable because its illusory existence may be jeopardized.

A chief feature is designed to be transformed through Self-remembering into something divine: your Self.

You must not be attracted to the problem, but to the solution.

It is not so much a matter of seeing the lower self, but of concentrating on Presence.

Imagination is the most difficult negative feature to control. One will awaken to find the 'I's in imagination about the work.

Vanity in one's machine can feign Self-remembering. Ironically, one can add to one's false personality if one acquires the *act* of Self-remembering rather than Self-remembering itself.

Higher Centers enjoy the quiet moment and restful impressions.

False personality craves novelty. It seeks one new thing after another rather than being content with the simplicity of Self-remembering. David must slay Goliath. Esoterically, Goliath is false personality and David, World 6.

Novelty produces Higher Centers, and yet a man number four cannot rely upon novelty to create a permanent level of consciousness.

The lower self actively looks for things to criticize in itself and others.

Self-judgment is the principal weapon of the lower self.

The fact that the lower self is so active at judging shows that it is one of its most effective weapons.

One reason we succumb to judgment and keeping accounts is that we are often right about what we are judging. However, the higher right is to disallow judgment and to transform it into Presence.

Never take any lower self personally. They are all the same, although they think they are all different. One can recognize some of one's lower self in everyone, and if one does not judge, one remains one's Higher Self.

Never judge, just observe.

People do not need to be judged; they need to be helped, as we are being helped by Influence C.

One should not compare one's progress with another's.

To evolve, one must learn from others rather than compete with them.

Self-deprecation is a waste of time; this too is not Self-remembering.

Externally considering others helps one confront self-deprecation.

We still have not gotten to the bottom of things as long as we are blaming someone else; neither are we ourselves to blame. That, too, is not Self-remembering.

The attempt to remember one's Self is not Self-remembering. The words "Be present" are not the state, although that precious phrase is dear to us in our aim to awaken.

The words "I am here" are only a stepping-stone to the presence of Higher Centers.

Disappointment with one's efforts is just another negative emotion.

If you have a negative emotion and your Third Eye is observing it, you are not the negative emotion.

Sometimes we pass through a trial and we fail. We must remember that, even though we have lost a battle, it is preparation for winning the war against sleep.

It is important to learn from your mistakes but not to dwell on them.

Through a thousand mistakes, one is born.

One cannot arrive at wordless Presence without giving up all that appears to be Presence.

Eventually the Third Eye will win out over the lower self.

CHAPTER 7

Tempted by Relative Awakening

As a young teacher I said that schools are not for partial awakening.... One cannot keep both one's Higher Centers and one's lower self – one of them has to go.

Being content with relative awakening is a dangerous attitude that one must control. Schools are not designed for relative awakening; they are designed for complete awakening. Influence B is relative awakening and relies upon symbols of identity rather than awakening itself.

One must be careful not to think one has more than one has. Relative awakening is insufficient compared with being awake. One can descend and not know it.

The whole task of one's life is to occupy oneself with pursuing the right issue, because there are ten thousand seemingly attractive things one can do with one's life, which are all meaningless without Presence.

One of the dangers of relative awakening is that it is higher than life.

It is a dead end if one cannot be what one talks about.

One loses one's Soul to blind faith. In schools one's faith is a result of one's verifications.

If one's aims are connected with Self-remembering, one's activities will not pose a problem. A man number four thinks that he can accommodate deviations within his aim to awaken, but awakening does not allow for many mechanical *cul-de-sacs*; one is allotted a limited amount of time to learn a lesson.

Because it cannot arrive at the present, the lower self wants to remain at the level of the magnetic center.

What is it one has accepted instead of one's Soul?

Student: What is the greatest danger in awakening? To seek power over others rather than oneself. Power over people is a buffer to power over oneself.

The only position of authority one should seek is Divine Presence controlling the lower self – this state controlling imagination.

The machine wants answers that keep one asleep.

Do not look for a different answer. Look for the same answer by going deeper: wordless Presence.

If one's life does not revolve around Presence, it revolves around sleep. Sleep is the essence of life for unconscious man. Presence is the essence of life for conscious man.

Sleep is not innocent – it is a lack of effort.

Sleep is broken by Presence.

A student's instinctive center will try to sever his relationship with the Teacher or the school, as a way of severing the relationship with his own Higher Centers. The instinctive center tries to separate Self-remembering from the presence of the Teacher and the school and thus destroy it by isolation.

The only real death is losing Influence C. Other than this there is no death for ascending Souls in schools.

Try to allow for being weary of the struggle. It will pass.

PART III

THE ROLE OF HIGHER FORCES IN AWAKENING HIGHER CENTERS

The most important factor in awakening is having Influence C touch one's shoulder and allow one to evolve.

No one can escape without outside help; sacred messengers are required to put the necessary pressure on us that we could not put on ourselves.

Awakening, including the entire concept, comes from the gods.

One can only know and be whatever Influence C allow.

The appearance of Higher Centers is the result of an accumulated effort. Each of our machines wastes opportunities because the areas of friction that higher forces select are considered too sacred by false personality. If friction is not given where identifications exist, one would remain a machine. One cannot remember one's Self sufficiently without higher forces intervening to arrange suffering.

Without the outside help of Influence C – visible or invisible – it is not possible to distinguish consciousness from functions.

Influence C have a keen desire to help anyone who wishes to awaken.

We do not need to hope that some higher power is hearing us. In fact, higher forces are producing us.

CHAPTER 8

Chosen to Evolve

Awakening is unrelated to age, gender, or race. What matters is being chosen to evolve by Influence C. It is not one's physical body that was chosen to evolve, but one's Higher Centers.

One starts to evolve at the pace of higher forces when Higher Centers begin to appear, that is, at the speed of light.

The reason we were chosen is because we worked on inducing consciousness in previous lives. Predestined luck – we had it before we were conceived. The more present we are, the more our luck increases.

Influence C design our luck over the course of nine lifetimes. One life is not sufficient for immortality, but nine lives are.

Each life is an illusory setting for Divine Presence.

At no time are we ever the physical body; we are Third Eye, which passes through nine lives.

Your former lives were not as important as your present life, nor is your present life as important as your ninth life.

If you could see the play of your lives you would not be identified with the present one.

Focus on the present and let lifetimes and numbers take care of themselves.

The gods, in silence, observe your tendencies, especially the sacred desire to awaken and evolve.

People do not know what to look for. One must be trained by Influence C regarding what to seek and how to vanquish imagination.

Each of our roles is written by higher forces expressly for awakening.

Influence C have placed us wherever is best for our evolution.

We have to pretend that we do everything. At the same time, we all have a predestined play to become present.

Student: Could angles be shared on the apparent contradiction that we are in a play, and that we must take responsibility for our actions? These two relative thoughts on the subject of one's life are not opposed to each other. One is a machine, and a most unusual machine because one can experience immortal states. If one is attempting to Self-remember and C Influence is assisting one, there are two positive forces in one's favor. "One has fate" means that any significant action of one's life is monitored by higher forces. When one understands the concept of fate, one should not enter tramp by refusing to take responsibility for one's actions, as higher forces are not always with one.

Man is quite unaware of the extent to which everything on earth is monitored by Influence C.

Everything in the play of humanity and schools was in order before the earth was even created.

Angels have been with you always. They were with you before you were born and they will stay with you until you become as they are – immortal.

When one finds Influence C, one stops looking and eventually becomes like them.

The further we go with Influence C, the luckier we become.

CHAPTER 9

Out of the Mud...the Lotus

Out of the mud, friction, grows the lotus of Higher Centers.

Friction is the struggle between Presence and sleep.

One's Self would perish without friction as friction is nourishment for Higher Centers.

When friction is very intense, one may forget that it is a play; when it subsides one realizes the shock was to develop Higher Centers. Influence C have scripted everything, including all the opposition to Presence. Unwittingly, the lower self participates in this process. We evolve not in spite of, but because of, friction.

The more one starts to awaken, the more bizarre the 'I's Influence C give one as they jolt the Ruling Faculty, producing Higher Centers.

As you develop, you will experience sudden bursts of negative 'I's that the lower self sends forth. You have to pull back and say *"Drop."* Influence C control these 'I's and that is how they awaken one.

Through trials, try to maintain a high standard of Self-remembering. A strong shock will not vanish; it leaves the Third State of consciousness resounding in one.

Because Self-remembering is self-defense, one can deal with brutal shocks simply by holding on to one's work.

Self-remembering takes care of everything.

All men number four, five, six, and seven require friction to keep their work practical and to change their level of being.

A real teacher is on the front burner and real students are on the other burners getting sautéed.

There is no easy way to Higher Centers. Whether one awakens in the East or in the West, one's trials are difficult: Buddha and Socrates both died of poison. Distinguished men are martyred so that humanity will cultivate the principles which these men uphold.

Transformation of real suffering creates real Presence.

Unnecessary suffering is sustained primarily through identification and a poorly established sense of scale. . . . Real suffering pierces imaginary suffering and stills us.

When you do not understand something, it invariably reveals a lack of scale and relativity.

One cannot discriminate unless one establishes scale, and one cannot establish scale without transforming large suffering.

Self-remembering is the summit of scale.

When you have angels in your life, you can think on the right scale.

When one experiences suffering, a useful work 'I' is: "Remember not to waste Influence C's work."

Influence C are not cruel. One is a machine, asleep, under feminine dominance, so they give one what one needs to escape. Usually all they ask is that we transform identification.

Friction is proof that Influence C love us.

Never doubt that the gods love you, even though they crush you into being to awaken you.

Like wine, one must be crushed, fermented, and aged.

Influence C push us to our means by pushing us beyond our means.

Influence C's methods to awaken you are like the weather, which can be bitterly cold or incredibly hot. There is nothing one can do but endure.

Even C Influence have a dualistic nature: they carry a wand in one hand and a club in the other.

Nothing is sacred to Influence C except one's Self.

Whatever shocks Influence C give us are necessary for our

evolution. Shocks freeze us in Presence. The speechless state they create is who we are.

Man number four is often given blunt shocks because subtle shocks pass by unnoticed.

Shocks are often the third force to catapult us into the present. Influence C will sometimes create the Third State by subtle extremes, such as being served the smallest or largest glass of water in one's life.

Shocks enable you to know your Self; transforming them enables you to be your Self.

We always need what we are given whether it be a pleasant experience or rough friction.

One of the major hallmarks of Self-remembering is that it works with the defect of the moment.

If you are having trouble remembering your Self, keep trying. It is all we can do. Self-remembering is always right action.

Eventually, one accepts shocks not as interruptions in one's life, but, thankfully, as interruptions in one's sleep, and values them for bringing forth Higher Centers.

CHAPTER 10

Conscious Offspring

Only the Absolute evolved without help. The Absolute is a universe of conscious love. We are His conscious offspring.

Our little Higher Centers are a gift from the Absolute. By creating the universe, the Absolute very generously gave ascending Souls the opportunity to realize His mystery within themselves.

World 1 is the Absolute; World 3 is his Higher Emotional Center; World 6 is our Higher Mental Center; World 12 is our Higher Emotional Center; and World 24 is the nine of hearts in essence Presence form.

The Absolute created the universe in order to produce the state of Divine Presence in the microcosmos man or woman. It is totally irrelevant whether you are male or female or black or white because consciousness is not functions.

Through Self-remembering we experience sublime Cosmic Consciousness; our cosmos is awake rather than asleep.

Third Eye is an immortal work of art; it is the greatest achievement of the Absolute.

The key to understanding the scriptures is to realize that God is not an external deity, but one's own Presence. In schools, God is the divinity within – the state we are in.

The divinity within you is the only figure that has the right to use the word 'I'. "God" always refers to the divinity within, not to the Absolute without. It is amazing grace that He has allowed us to share the same state that He has.

The figure most interested in evolution is the Absolute, followed by the most ancient angels.

Angels are men who have transcended themselves – they are far more beautiful than man can conceive.

Because angels can manage anything necessary on earth, the Absolute's direct influence does not reach us. Angels thrive on being externally considerate; it is a permanent state for them. We are stones that they have brought to life, and, although we are their children, man-sized results are expected of us.

Presence is an angel's view. Angels have an altogether different level of vision that we do not comprehend.

Higher Centers are the angel within.

Presence is produced by Influence C's efforts and our own.

Influence C cannot be present for us. They can arrange the right circumstances, but they want us to be present for ourselves.

Influence C are immeasurably devoted to you. You are their conscious offspring.

Even though they are more advanced, Influence C's story is our story.

Student: How do you see us? As angels in their infancy. Outside the Celestial City of Paradise you are the most precious beings that exist – angels in gestation.

Remember that we are changing from being machines to becoming angels. That is why awakening is called "the impossible dream."

Presence is a divine state which belongs to Paradise. It is placed in the human body to strengthen itself.

We are here to strengthen the conscious child within.

When you are present, Influence C have company.

CHAPTER 11

Attracting Higher Forces

When our little Higher Centers are wide awake, we are a gentle fragrance, attracting higher forces to pollinate us.

We are more receptive to Influence C when we are in essence. In personality we deflect; in essence we absorb.

The most important thing is to locate Influence C and to stay with them.

One's own Third Eye is conscious influence within. You are your own church or temple when you are present.

Third Eye is a wireless connection with Influence C.

Influence C whisper answers to us that should enable us to be present and control the lower self.

Everything is whispering "Be," if only we are alert to it.

We are in touch with the miraculous – both internally and externally. When doing business with Influence C, Self-remembering comes first, external results second.

Influence C move fast. Be responsive and ready.

One way you can start verifying Influence C is that too many things will happen that cannot be ascribed to accident. However, with verification, you do not want to be too eager to accept Influence C, or to reject them. Just be open and neutral.

One verifies Influence C through the transformation of suffering.

Our verifications must be deep enough to retain Influence C in our lives.

Once Influence C have revealed themselves to you, it is important to strengthen this connection for the rest of your lives.

You must try to find out what the immortal gods want for the school and for oneself, and lay aside one's own instinctive willfulness. The school must have a form that feeds Paradise – it cannot be earthbound. By being willful, one creates one's own imaginary denying force.

The lower self creates a network of buffers in order to reject assistance from Influence C.

It is imperative to develop a proper attitude towards one's teacher because a teacher is the bridge between school on earth and higher school.

I am a conscious teacher and I know how to bring your Soul into being.

The Teacher is Influence C.

As a teacher, the gods have given me the gift of awakening and they wish me to share it with you. The role of the teacher is to be an island of love for his students.

I am a link between heaven and earth. I am both one of you and one of them.

My job is to get you to understand what I understand, what I have received from higher school.

The gods need the Absolute's will. I need Influence C's will, and students need my will to escape.

School events are our opportunity to help Influence C and, therefore, the Absolute. They are when our Presence is the strongest. The more one helps Influence C, the more they will help one.

Student: Can one have Influence C outside of schools? Individuals are awakened by Influence C, but on their own divine terms. I awakened without school knowledge.

On Sept. 5, 1967, I met Alex Horn. This date marks the moment when I met Influence C; it was the first flash of consciousness. The first time I met Alex Horn made such a strong impression on me that afterwards I just kept walking in the night. My Higher Centers were whirling. In just under ten years, my Higher Centers became permanent.

When Higher Centers are working, in most instances Influence C are with one.

The closer you draw to Influence C, the closer you draw to your Self.

Influence C have delivered the conscious child to us.

One must strive for the highest in one's Self to see the highest in others and Influence C.

One of the aspects of awakening is that there is no competitiveness; everyone is making efforts for himself and for the school. It is one for all and all for one.

It comes down to whether or not you have angels in your life, and we do.

Images of angels are the highest symbols of invisible Influence C. We actually have guardian angels guarding our Presence. Everything is real for us, not just symbolic.

Wherever you walk, anywhere in the world, an angel is hovering over you. Do not ever forget this.

PART IV

THE QUEST FOR PRESENCE –
THE STRUGGLE OF THE MAGICIANS

The greatest contradiction in nature is that of the Higher Self and the lower self temporarily cohabiting the same body. From this comes "The Struggle of the Magicians." It is a very necessary irritant.

We are engaged in a psychological battle to establish Presence over imagination.

You have to examine what takes the place of Self-remembering and experience an internal civil war.

The internal civil war between Self-remembering and sleep is the only battle worth fighting.

Everyone appears in this life in a vessel that is asleep. But the vessel carries a Third Eye that can awaken. Our first quest is to bring Presence and our second is to make it permanent.

The quest is always for Third Eye to be present.

Once one gets the habit of Self-remembering, nothing is wasted.

The trick is to keep Third Eye involved in everything one is doing.

CHAPTER 12

The Steward and the White Queen

The earth is a maximum security prison, and only the gods – the guardians – can let one know oneself. The gods have opened the vault for us, which allows us to pass from the steward to Higher Centers.

The steward is the priest of God – Third Eye.

It is the duty of the steward to induce Higher Centers to be present.

It is the steward's task to make something ordinary, extra-ordinary.

The steward is The Magician, Card I in the Tarot.

The instinctive center looks for opportunities to occupy space; the steward and Higher Centers must look for opportunities to displace the instinctive center.

A steward is designed into one's machine with limitations – it is not intended to control difficult situations as a certain intensity is needed to produce Higher Centers.

One cannot have wordless Presence without control of the passions.

If the steward is weak, then the Third Eye will be weak.

Very discreetly, the nine of hearts does all the work, while the steward receives all the credit. In fact, the steward is a guise for the nine of hearts.

"Behind every great man . . . is a great woman" – Isis, Athena, Mary: the nine of hearts.

Ouspensky said that the work must be emotional. This refers to the nine of hearts reaching, contacting Higher Emotional Center.

The most powerful figure on the chessboard is not the white king, but the white queen – the nine of hearts.

The white queen is a great servant to Third Eye.

The white queen must engage and support Higher Emotional Center – World 12 – Third Eye. The nine of hearts is located in the heart; the Higher Emotional Center in the forehead.

The nine of hearts is the female counterpart of the Higher Emotional Center. The nine of hearts is the lower emotional center; the four wordless breaths are the Higher Emotional Center.

The nine of hearts transcends herself into the Higher Emotional Center.

It is necessary to distinguish between our king of hearts and our Higher Centers to ensure that we pass through the king of hearts into Presence, and not merely speak about it. There are beautiful treasures in the king of hearts, but Moses was denied the Promised Land. The steward does not become conscious; the Higher Centers become conscious.

The steward cannot look at the sun. Presence is reserved for Third Eye.

The strength of the steward is the ability to recede when the Master arrives.

One must train one's steward to consent silently to Presence whenever it arises.

Efforts to remember one's Self accrue and Higher Centers may crescendo for fifteen minutes before their ability to "Be" is exhausted. At such times one must return to one's steward, for he will prevent one from descending too far.

The steward is virtual reality and Higher Centers are reality itself.

The steward's job is to emulate what he sees in Presence.

It is useful to remember that no state is permanent for man number four, not even Self-remembering. This is why standards are necessary, as they prevent one from descending below them.

Higher Centers and lower centers – God and the steward – have a vigilant relationship.

CHAPTER 13

Work 'I's

Work 'I's connect the steward to Higher Centers.

Work 'I's are closer to the Third State of consciousness. Formatory 'I's are closer to the first state of consciousness.

Work 'I's pull one towards the Third Eye and away from the evil eye.

The thirty great work 'I's are different ways to close down the lower self and open up the Higher Self.[2]

Work 'I's remind Presence what to do with itself, and to not succumb to imagination.

"To be the words" means for the work 'I's to act and engage the state they are pointing to.

The many 'I's individually do not have a lot of strength. Work 'I's have the most strength – the strength to engage Presence.

Work 'I's turn denying force to our advantage.

---

2. The Appendix provides a complete list of the thirty great work 'I's.

The best work 'I' is the one that works.

I frequently use about ten to fifteen of the thirty work 'I's, such as: *Drop, Use, Kneel, Move, Taste, Look, Smell, Hear, Feel,* and *Pax.*

I use individual work 'I's more often than the sequence.

Student: Which work 'I's do you find most effective? Most times I do it directly from the Third Eye – occasionally, I use *Kneel* or *Pax.*

Drop is one of our greatest allies. Please make it the strongest of the individual work 'I's.

I often use *Pax* to work with impatience. As one gets older, the machine becomes more and more impatient. *Pax* controls the queens. *Student: I have used "Shush" successfully when working with the queens.* Try to use what all other schools have used – innovation comes from the lower self. Try to avoid a homemade approach.

When one reads with Presence one goes a little more slowly.

Look gives one the Third Eye perspective.

Child is another word for essence – a reminder to be in essence, not personality.

One of the easiest ways to be present is to listen.

When someone speaks, we often hear only one or two words and not the whole sentence, and then conclude something different than was intended. We need to use *Hear with Presence.*

The attitude one has towards listening can distort the wisdom one receives.

It is the most difficult of all things to engage Presence with a work 'I'. This is conscious, not mechanical, work.

There is a time to try to avoid all 'I's, even work 'I's. In proper order, words teach one to be silent.

CHAPTER 14

Enabling Grace – The Sequence

The sequence is a conscious order of creation that produces Divine Presence in the microcosmos man.

The sequence is an alarm that alerts Third Eye to awaken to itself.

The sequence is aimed directly at minimizing unnecessary talk.

The steward says *"Be,"* *"Hold,"* *(Theme),* *"Back,"* *(Theme),* *"BE."* The sequence was designed to help the Self remember itself – Self-remembering.

The most important thing is to intone the sequence from essence. For *Be* to act it must come from Presence – a state of essence aware of itself.

Behind the sequential mask lies the conscious child within.

The first part of the sequence is relative consciousness and the Four Wordless Breaths are full consciousness.

With the best sequences, Presence is equally strong both during and after the sequence – throughout the Ten Commandments. With other sequences Presence may only become strong when we reach long *BE*, while at other times we may lose Presence during the four wordless breaths. *Everything depends upon our desire to sincerely engage and prolong Presence with each sequence.*

If one says "*Be*" and Presence emerges, one does not need to say "*Hold*" until Presence begins to diminish. Consequently, the more successful one is, the slower one's use of the work 'I's will be.

The sequence must act or one remains veiled.

To make the sequence act, you must be emotional. The Higher Emotional Center must be engaged, supported by the nine of hearts.

Unveiling is Presence, and through a sequence we unveil. This echoes something I said a long time ago, "Removing what is not Self-remembering requires Self-remembering."

The sequence detects both the Higher Self and the lower self.

As one's ability to use the sequence increases, one's capacity to detect the lower self will also increase.

For the sequence to have any value, it must complete itself. Some sequences are preparation for becoming more serious about completing them.

The lower self will criticize a sequence that is not perfect. Discard that.

The pyramid represents the sequence, and its task is to engage Divine Presence.

Pyramids are an esoteric symbol of the creation of Higher Centers.

"At the still point" – the top of the pyramid, long *BE* – "there the dance is" – the Four Wordless Breaths.

When the top of a pyramid is cut off, it means that long *BE* has transcended itself in Divine Presence.

A student asked me when he should use the sequence, and I replied, "Whenever you need it."

Only when we reach firm Presence are we secure.

The sequence is often best when we are alone because when we are together, we help each other to be present. When we are alone, it is the Third Eye against the lower self; however, when we are together, if we are doing our work, we strengthen one another.

The sequence is the path to Presence. We have never been so present, so often, and for so long, as with the sequence.

For forty years our school kept going forward, until we finally arrived at the greatest ally of Presence – the sequence.

CHAPTER 15

Amazing Grace

The first part of the sequence is "enabling grace" and then you have "amazing grace" – wordless Presence. Six is human and four is Divine.

The whole point of the sequence is to engage magic. Third Eye must appear at each step, and then you combust into consciousness without functions – magic.

One trades the intonation of the sequence by the nine of hearts for a garden – for Third Eye.

When entering a garden try to be especially present, because symbolically one is in the realm of the Four Wordless Breaths. Mohammed said, "When you see a Garden of Paradise, roam in it."

The four wordless breaths are consciousness without functions, Presence without words, and are the very heart of this school, and of all schools; it actually happens up here, in the Third Eye.

Only Real 'I' can know itself and witness the inhalation and exhalation of the four wordless breaths.

The four wordless breaths are "God-Realization," which brings to an end the lower self's shadowy resistance to our sequence.

The "Promised Land" is the kingdom of heaven – the Third State. It is not for *Be, Hold, Hear, Back, Hear, BE*. It is not for Moses – the steward – it is for Third Eye.

Third Eye is the issue, not the sequence. Rumi said, "There is no miracle but seeing your own Beloved" – your own Third Eye. When the nine of hearts reaches *BE*, the Higher Emotional Center appears. Seeing long *BE*, the Third Eye is born, and conscious knowledge and light are born – the four wordless breaths.

Presence obliterates the sequence and the ten thousand 'I's.

A Zen Master said, "If even the sublime Dharma has to be relinquished, how much more so that which contradicts the Dharma?" If even the sequence must be relinquished, how much more so the ten thousand idiots?

During the Four Wordless Breaths, whenever possible do nothing else – just be present to your life.

There is nothing more practical than experiencing mystical states; they are the fruition of our daily efforts. When you are present, allow the state to circulate throughout your being.

The highest achievement is reaching Presence without words – consciousness without functions. All religions of the world are pointing to this.

CHAPTER 16

Using the Arts for Consciousness

You can use any of the arts to make your Self more conscious.

The arts must lead to Presence; otherwise they have no value for either the viewer or the listener.

Beautiful impressions, whether natural or man-made, function as a catalyst for Higher Centers. This is why it is important to be in good householder – an unkempt environment repels rather than attracts Higher Centers.

The senses are needed to produce Higher Centers. Looking at nature or listening to music can evoke Higher Centers.

Beautiful impressions invite Presence. Negative impressions lead us to the transformation of negativity.

Impressions are truly Soul food.

We help one another when we point out beautiful impressions in the present.

Dull impressions evoke mechanical reactions while quality impressions in small items such as wallets, watches, pens, etc. are more likely to evoke Self-remembering. As one handles these items all of one's life, one will find they serve as a useful shock as they increase positive force (first force).

It is important to be quiet and absorbent, especially around beautiful impressions. In this way one brings everything one has learned in one's life to the present. We must absorb nature, not deflect it through false personality.

When looking at art, one has to be patient and keep looking through Presence, and the answers will come. Awe in art must be accompanied by Presence. What observes – the Third Eye – will always be greater than what is observed.

No great palace with great art can compare with great Presence.

We look at these images with Presence – with the Astral Body, which is altogether different than the physical body.

All conscious art was created with Presence and is meant to be viewed with Presence. It is school work to view objects with Presence.

When one looks at school works with Presence, the Third Eye is looking at a symbol of itself. When the Third Eye understands a symbol of itself, it strengthens itself.

Look for the divine element in art, even in simple or coarse objects.

We are unique in making these pilgrimages to temples of art to strengthen our king of hearts and, more so, the Presence of Third Eye. In museums or temples, one must walk with the

Third Eye and not merely with the moving center in order to receive the messages.

There is no higher art form than reality, which is Higher Centers within one.

Museums are houses of sacred answers. Museums enable us to collect Presence because, if we pursue the message in a museum, it produces Presence.

It is a more beautiful experience to look at these objects with one another in museums than by ourselves – many shared thoughts come together.

When the art is great it will help you to produce your Soul and, curiously, also when it is bad. The Sistine Chapel, for example, is great art that helps you to produce your Soul. Something bad could have a similar effect. That is the beauty of the arts.

Art does not have to be beautiful to have the message. I used to think that the answer was exquisite art, but then I found out that objects very poorly made can have the same great inner meaning.

The art of Mesoamerica is often very primitive, but the message is very sophisticated. It matters little how the message was painted or sculpted, compared to actually living it.

We used to study art from the merely aesthetic point of view. With the keys, it is a much more intelligent experience; it instructs our Higher Centers to *BE*.

Before receiving the keys, we knew to look with Presence, but we did not know that virtually everything we were looking at had information to instruct Presence.

We have been given the keys to the Bible to help us work with things that others have worked with before us. They had to keep their knowledge in keys because they could not speak the truth openly – but they too had sacred messengers helping them. We are fighting and winning the same battle they fought and won.

To understand the keys one must realize that the different gods of the same religion represent the various characteristics of the steward, nine of hearts, or Presence.

 The Sphinx, the pharaoh, Moses, Christ, Mary, Mohammed, Nefertiti, Isis, and Athena all represent the nine of hearts, or characteristics of the nine of hearts, supporting the Four Wordless Breaths.

Artists often make the nine of hearts quite plain so that she does not compete with the beauty of the Higher Emotional Center.

Tarot Card XXI – the Higher Emotional Center – is the most beautiful woman in the world.

One cannot see hidden symbols in art, nor create them, without Influence C. The challenge for any artist is to portray the invisible and to express the inexpressible.

A real painter must materialize World 12 in himself while painting. The canvas is a mirror for the state.

One can be a great artist and have the system, yet it must be in right order: to have the system and then art.

The ability to portray the message well does not necessarily translate into the capacity to be it, to transcend it into Presence.

When studying the message, one must look for what the artist expressed, not for what one wishes to see. The lower self looks for its idea of the message so that it can take credit for it.

Sensitivity to the circle and the square makes it possible to understand all schools.

The triangle is the sequence; the circle is the sequence completing itself; and the square is the Four Wordless Breaths.

Naturally one looks for the message to be depicted in the more obvious parts of the body, such as the face or torso. Schools often express ideas in a more subtle way, and one finds messages in the passive space or in the feet of a sculpture.

It is the most challenging task to portray the invisible nature of higher mind. How do we paint the invisible? How do we sculpt the invisible? Artists often do it by placing an empty square in their sculptures or paintings.

The passive space is the same as the wordless place. The nine of hearts keeps wordless Presence empty of words. Schools teach this through the empty space.

Both the ballet and the music that accompanies it are wordless, as is the Divine Presence that beholds it.

The message in ballet is thorough, deep, and enchanting – the human body is used as a living medium to express a wordless message.

The hummingbird was a symbol of Third Eye for the Meso-americans. The swan is an inner concept, representing wordless Presence.

You must neither fall in love with, nor be repelled by, the form of the message because either reaction is a deception of the lower self, designed to prevent us from understanding the message.

One can find the message, but to unlock its secrets, one must be in essence. It is one thing to have the message and another to utilize it correctly. The key is to stay in essence.

The state we are in, essence aware of itself, is very simple. That is why simple images are so often favored by Presence itself.

Esoteric images are only symbols of what you possess.

The Sphinx represents the steward looking up to God – the four wordless breaths – not the external God – the author of the universe, but Higher Mental and Emotional Centers in the microcosmos man. When we say "the microcosmos man," we mean both man and woman.

To understand what the Sphinx represents is an incomplete experience. To achieve it oneself and to internalize Presence is a complete experience.

Robert Earl Burton (2016)

PART V

THE QUEST TO MAKE PRESENCE PERMANENT

All of our moments of Presence eventually lead to solid Presence. Consciousness has degrees and one of the degrees is that it is permanent.

No one has done enough until Presence is made permanent.

We are all blessed spirits, blessed by angels. It just takes time to make it permanent.

The Soul is composed of an imperishable substance that becomes permanent. Like the fragrance of a rose, we cannot see it, yet it is there. It is molecular.

CHAPTER 17

Sustaining Presence

Presence must sustain itself.

Prolonged Presence is strength from above. All 'I's that oppose this state will be mastered by this state.

The Higher Centers mold the intellectual parts of centers to promote and prolong Presence.

In the state of Presence you learn to shape the thirty work 'I's that help you to remain present.

The intellectual parts of centers must accustom themselves to continually assert the one-syllable work 'I's. Once this habit has been acquired, the work 'I's assist Divine Presence and Divine Presence the work 'I's; they mutually support each other. Here, then, is a way of prolonging Presence.

When you use the thirty work 'I's intermittently, your favorite subject of imagination will continue to intrude. However, with practice the work 'I's will appear more and more often, and will lift you out of imagination more frequently.

Follow one work 'I' with another work 'I' until the capstone, perfect Presence, is in place.

When you have engaged Divine Presence, do not be curious about things unrelated to prolonging Presence, lest you fall into imagination.

To sustain Higher Centers one must be able to control lying in the four lower centers.

Hydrogens 6 and 12 are clinical labels for one's embryonic Soul. Each time we suffer a shock we produce a trace of this imperishable, divine substance. Apollo ruling the four horses that pull his chariot esoterically refers to World 6 controlling the four lower centers.

The more you prolong Presence, the more hostility you will encounter from the lower self.

One must continue to work on what one knows is not Self-remembering because what is not Self-remembering tries relentlessly to undermine what truly is Self-remembering.

One of the best ways to remember yourself is to remove what is not Self-remembering. Here nature plays a trick in our favor because an expression of Self-remembering is required to remove what is not Self-remembering.

Presence is not negative, not indignant, not irreverent. Presence does not think of itself as important. Presence reaches itself and sustains itself by avoiding these pitfalls.

When you are present, you must find ways to increase endurance.

Shocks will introduce higher states, and transforming shocks will prolong them.

The sequence is either for retrieving Presence from imagination or for strengthening Presence.

When the Third Eye realizes that it has been in imagination, it pulls away from the lower self and begins a sequence coming from Presence.

Third Eye constantly tries to renew itself with individual work 'I's or with a sequence.

The Higher Centers encourage the steward to rise from imagination and promote Presence. In almost all cases, the word "*Be*" issues from the Higher Centers to the steward.

The sequence coming from Presence is best. We are in the temple before we begin. Mohammed said, "When the call to prayer is heard it is better to already be in the temple." If we bring a sequence from Presence, we are already "in the temple." A firm sequence is a joyful experience.

Most of the Islamic patterns begin with a square that becomes two interlocking squares and then spirals into a circle, signifying that they are coming from Presence. We begin with a square – Presence – then we come to a circle – the sequence – so that the Third Eye can strengthen itself.

In his painting "God Creating the Universe," William Blake

makes a circle – the sun – and God in the form of a cube. This is a very nice way to see the idea of a sequence coming from Presence. It is coming from the Third Eye as a cube.... He is sending the sequence down like lightning, in short *Be* – long *BE* form. This is the greatest image in all schools for showing that a sequence coming from Presence is a square – a cube – the Third Eye.

Presence cannot be understood, yet even so the heart must sustain it.

If the Third Eye starts to wane, the heart must send an infusion of energy to sustain it.

If the heart does not refresh the Four Wordless Breaths, they will wilt.

The quality of Presence depends upon the strength and alertness of the Higher Centers, and also upon the capacity of the nine of hearts to support it.

At these events we do not need the sequence because we collectively strengthen each other. We inspire one another to be present without words for an hour.

We have pure minds right now, so we have "uncreated light"; the sequence is "created light."

The sequence and the Four Wordless Breaths are the most important experience in the universe, but what you have now [Presence during a meeting] transcends even that.

Prolonged Divine Presence is the uncreated activity of the divinity within. The Third Eye is doing everything it can to make itself last.

Presence stretches time, and eventually one extends time to the point of becoming immortal.

CHAPTER 18

Third Eye Educates Itself

As Higher Centers begin to function, they are naive little infants, and one is simply grateful for their arrival. Later the same state reads books and listens to music; it starts educating itself. I am not referring to educating essence, but to Higher Centers in connection with essence.

When one awakens, one needs to educate one's Higher Centers so that they can be of use to oneself and others.

Many ideas of the system can only be understood if one has had a legitimate experience with Higher Centers.

The knowledge we share is powerful because *reality is a foreign experience*. You understand this when you establish a brief connection with Higher Centers.

Knowledge of the system educates Third Eye.

The essence of knowledge is self-knowledge, and the essence of self-knowledge is Self-remembering.

Self-knowledge is the food of the Soul.

Fairy tales are very nutritious food for the Higher Emotional

Center. They begin in time – "Once upon a time" – and end in eternity – "and they lived happily ever after."

The development of intellectual parts of centers, the education of essence, is a necessary bridge to Higher Centers.

Being in the intellectual parts of centers strengthens the life of the Higher Centers.

When one begins to awaken one can strengthen an immature emotional center by appreciating subjects rather than identifying with them.

It is helpful to concentrate one's first line efforts on profound works dealing with the Ruling Faculty of man or Higher Centers. For example: *The Discourses of Epictetus*, *Meditations of Marcus Aurelius*, *Eckermann's Conversations with Goethe*, the *Sonnets of William Shakespeare*, and *Whitman's Leaves of Grass*. Johann Goethe, whom higher forces are using as a model of development for Apollo, suggested that every day one should read a good poem, view a fine painting, hear a little music, and where possible, speak a few reasonable words.

Unless one is looking for the inner meaning, study is of no use to Higher Centers.

The inner meaning is for Higher Centers, and the outer meaning is for the lower self. The inner meaning is for schools, and the outer meaning is for life.

To all those who understand it, the outer meaning has no meaning. It is merely a symbol of what should be achieved internally.

One does not begin by filling centers, one begins by short *Be* acting. This is the huge difference between life schools and conscious schools.

Schools are designed to accelerate your evolution – the faster you learn your lessons, the sooner you can receive more knowledge. School work frees the little child within from the bondage of the lower self.

It is our task to concentrate on Higher Centers more than on merely filling lower centers.

Life fills lower centers. Schools fill Higher Centers and foil death.

Enlightenment is not only about filling centers, but more importantly, about transcending them.

Second to second, one has to discern which part of oneself one is feeding: the Higher Self or the lower self.

Throughout one's life there are endless lessons without words that are designed to bypass one's intellectual center and reach one's Soul.

Luck is the Higher Emotional Center – the luck to recognize, value, and develop it.

Our Higher Centers are infants, but as the centuries pass they surely mature, retaining their innocence.

The sequence is baby food for the conscious infant within us. It nourishes our little Higher Centers.

One remains a student eternally, in this life and the next.

CHAPTER 19

On the Way

Man prefers allurement to reality, but students on the way realize that a certain practicality which is not in allurement is necessary to open Higher Centers.

Each person who enters the way creates a permanent tendency to evolve that passes from one life to another, and eventually becomes fully conscious in his or her ninth lifetime.

In most people, Higher Centers are but infants. People who enter the way, however, will experience Higher Centers in lucid durations of five, ten, or thirty minutes.

When one enters the way, the price, the privilege, and the payment are revealed.

Whether you are a woman or a man, the payment is the same.

When one enters the way, one's entire life eventually becomes an unremitting effort.

One cannot discount fate when considering the progress of one's evolution. People who enter the way have fate, which means that they can perform no more and no less in this lifetime than their roles dictate.

When you enter the way, you belong to the gods, who in turn ensure that you belong to your Self.

The idea of a fate designed to make one conscious must fall on the good householder within one and not on tramp. The good householder knows that extensive work is required throughout one's life in order to fulfill one's destiny.

One's work must become emotional and all who enter the way become emotional by penetrating essence, which is independent of one's center of gravity.

The production of Higher Centers is dependent on effort and conscious fate. Higher Centers themselves try to avoid the ever-prevalent law of accident.

One's Self, remembering, frees one from the law of accident.

The more you remember your Self, the more you are able to remember your Self because Self-remembering is a cumulative process.

Frequency of Self-remembering adds depth to Self-remembering.

The new man is born at the expense of the old – that is, at the expense of the king of clubs and the queen of hearts.

The old man in us is mechanical. The new man is conscious.

The old man is unconscious and does not know it. The new man is conscious and knows it.

When Higher Centers manifest, false personality will question the phenomenon since its existence is threatened by the birth of one's conscious faculties. One is a new being or a new man.

The more one focuses on school material, the more the old unconscious man is left behind.

Wordless Presence is the language of the new man.

Each conscious being began his evolution as a mechanical man; that is, as a man number one, two, or three.

Man number four differs from men number one, two, and three in that he knows he is asleep.

Everyone has a non-existence feature in relation to Self-remembering – when we are not remembering ourselves, we are all men number zero.

Higher Centers for a man number four, and less so for man number five, are as a dim light in the distance.

A man number four can periodically experience the being of a man number five, although he cannot sustain this level.

If you want to awaken, nothing will stand in your way; if you do not want to awaken, you will stand in your way.

One factor which separates a man number five from a man number four is that a man number five does not delay. He acts within the second, if possible, to promote an octave.

It takes more to awaken than we realize. Great personal effort is needed and Influence C must help one. The teacher must be conscious, the students must wish to help other students awaken, and one must have luck. One must be a healthy seed. One needs to have quite a discipline to awaken, a patience, an industriousness.

The more awake one becomes, the more offended one is by one's own unconscious manifestations. You will be upset about them in a positive, constructive way. If one is not offended by sleep, one will remain asleep.

What do we need to escape? Being. What prevents us from acquiring it? Lack of effort.

It is an inescapable fact that results will be proportional to effort.

One needs to learn to value "being" because that is what the next question is directing itself towards in some manner.

One must work beyond one's level of being to change one's level of being.

Knowledge and being must grow simultaneously.

The more one Self-remembers, the more one raises one's level and the more one starts to see Influence C speaking through others, oneself, and the Teacher.

One must patiently allow for time to align one's being with one's knowledge.

When one changes one's level of being, one becomes more of one's Self each time.

It is a law that one cannot see beyond one's level of being.

One understands from a higher school what one's level of being allows.

To see more one has to be more.

One cannot awaken unless one has verified that one is asleep; the absence of one's Self then increases valuation for it. Inevitably, one must reach the point of realizing that one is going to have to work to awaken, and that it is not going to just happen to one. The work is a labor of patience and eventually must permeate one's being.

Your Presence is a result of your verifications. Also, your verifications are a result of your Presence.

Periods of stagnation generally herald a breakthrough to a new level of being. One must endure them to advance.

Recognizing an interval as such is one of the best ways to bridge it.

A change in level of being does not occur all at once. One must bridge stagnant places within oneself and verify the ideas of the System to produce the courage to go on. If one makes efforts consistently, each day will take care of itself. The System works only if one uses it.

The more one changes one's level, the more invisible one becomes. One no longer needs symbols of identity because one has identity itself.

Now we have a Self to remember.

CHAPTER 20

Becoming a Conscious Being

To be a conscious being all you need to do is relinquish imagination for Presence. And that is most difficult which seems easiest – to insert this state above the second state.

To awaken, essentially one has to take everything before one as an opportunity for Presence.

With Presence, one does not need to pretend to be anything – one just needs to be one's Self. This state known to itself is the seal of a conscious being.

In order to be a conscious being, essence must transcend itself into Third Eye.

No one becomes a conscious being without Influence C's assistance. One cannot do it by oneself.

Student: Is it realistic to expect to become conscious in this life? It is realistic to try to be present in this life. When you are remembering yourself you are a conscious being, and the miraculous laws of higher worlds have appeared on your earth.

Some people awaken because they imagine it can be done, whereas others do not because they imagine it cannot.

People want consciousness to be mechanical goodness. Ascending Souls must often go against the tide of mechanical goodness to arrive at their destination and become conscious beings.

In my life, if I saw that there was something I could have done better, I made a mental note of it, and tried to do it better the next time. And so one eventually becomes a conscious being.

Student: Is there any one thing one can do to awaken? Yes, transform inconspicuous voluntary suffering daily.

Letting go of your negative emotions is voluntary suffering.

In order to awaken you must learn to do what the machine does not wish to do. This idea is a major element of awakening – it must also become a way of life.

Effort must become a way of life if one is to change one's level of being.

The three pillars of awakening are Self-remembering, Divided Attention, and the non-expression of negative emotions.

The transformation of suffering is still the principal way we escape.

The pearl of great price – one's Soul – is produced through the constant transformation of suffering.

To evolve one must transform the little negative events that occur each day; one can overcome great suffering only by transforming small sufferings.

All conscious beings and ascending Souls epitomize the transformation of suffering. The path to Presence is through the transformation of suffering. By transforming suffering you produce the conscious child within.

The aim is not to suffer; everyone suffers. The aim is to transform suffering into an Astral Body.

Being present leads to crystallization of an Astral Body, the formation of an immortal Soul.

We use the physical body to produce the Astral Body – the hidden meaning of the physical body is to produce your Third Eye.

Everyone is born with an Astral Body in an initial form. Only schools develop this "God particle" to full consciousness.

We have an Astral Body, but right now, in this earthly body, we can only sense Third Eye.

Presence is designed to be forever; great patience is required to crystallize this state.

Crystallization is an unbelievably real experience.

When I crystallized there was a flash of lightning, followed by smoke and a roll of unearthly thunder. The Higher Centers fused. My World 6 looked upon the event like the Sphinx, completely unperturbed. I realized then that it was impossible to destroy my Higher Centers. They are immortal.

During my crystallization, Higher Mental rather than Higher

Emotional handled the experience. It was not even a test; Higher Mental just went right through it. There was no question of failure.

After I crystallized, my first 'I' was "It worked!" Now I can say that it is working for all of you.

Student: What did your Higher Centers gain after crystallizing that they did not have before? Permanence. There were still many lessons to follow. Presence actually never stops learning.

One can never really stop making efforts. Even after crystallizing, Presence does not happen by itself.

Real Presence from Higher Centers is very rare, even in conscious beings.

Awakening means taking away what is not You until your last breath.

One never stops needing patience and the nearer one is to the goal, the more patience is needed.

Whatever you do, try to do it with as much Presence as you can, for in the end, that is all that truly matters.

I have opened Pandora's box for my students with the understanding that they can realize themselves. The System would fail if the Teacher could not withdraw his influence and allow his students to generate their own third force. Influence C intends to make one responsible for oneself by pushing one to the point where one must work alone.

PART VI
EMITTING DIVINE LIGHT

One must make maximum effort to emit and to receive divine light.

One receives light in one's youth and emits it in one's old age.

Schools represent conscious light on the earth. Love and light mean the same thing.

Third Eye wishes to express itself.

CHAPTER 21

Schools and the Message

The conscious aspects of the Ray of Creation must grow, and this is why schools exist.

Schools represent the Soul or pineal gland of humanity.

Schools focus on controlling the instinctive center and being present.

Wordless Presence aware of itself is a lesson seldom taught by Influence C, and it is only taught in schools.

Schools produce alerting awakening messages.

The sequence and Presence are the message within every message.

Wherever we go throughout the world we see the same great message producing the same incredible vibrant state.

Only schools can recognize schools because they possess the same message and the same state.

Schools never tire of the same message as it cures the same problem – sleep.

A practical school produces Higher Centers in its students.

Our school revived the message to the extent that it produces consciousness in everyone.

When you decipher the message, it produces Third Eye.

When Third Eye understands the message, it rises into being.

For the message to have value, you must be accompanied by Influence C.

It always takes Influence C to create the message, and it always takes Influence C to understand it.

Every age receives Influence C's blessing; the thread of schools is virtually unbroken. All schools together form a single mystery – wordless Presence. The only reason that the same message has been used for millennia is because it works, delivering us to Divine Presence.

All schools work, in that they all produce consciousness. What differs is the outer form.

The inner meaning of all religions is the same – the same religion coming from the same source: higher school.

Schools enact the inner meaning of all Holy Scriptures, while life enacts the outer meaning.

Doing the outer meaning kills the Third Eye.

Throughout the history of humanity, in all the traditions and what they left behind, amidst all the different forms and decorations, the message and the answer is You.

Schools are for the conscious child within us.

Every school uses a child to represent essence Presence. Many people are in essence, but it is only in schools that one finds pure essence aware of itself. It requires Influence C to take essence up to Presence.

Every school stays as close as possible to all the other schools that preceded it. Throughout history, all that has changed is the way in which the message was presented – the essence of the message has remained the same.

Influence C arranged for the system to be formulated by prehistoric man, by a culture without an alphabet, because the aim of the system is to strengthen the Higher Centers and not the lower functions. You can do both. In fact, most schools do both, but they always put Presence first.

Egypt is ultimate mysticism. It left its signature on all subsequent schools. Of course, everything Egypt became was inherited from the prehistoric tradition.

The system did not originate in Egypt, but it was perfected there.

Each school works with the same message, but it creates a unique, outstanding version of the message that is different from other schools.

Egypt set the tone for all schools to follow.

Incorporating the message was foremost for all schools and their artists.

Schools like to keep the message simple, then repeat and repeat and repeat, so that, as it slowly penetrates their being, students will understand it.

We need to hear the message over and over until we become the living answer. Presence never becomes tired of hearing a message that strengthens itself.

Schools often think in a cacophonous way, which breaks formatory mind. This goes against our usual training before the school, but we need to begin thinking in a new way.

We must bypass formatory mind in order to understand the esoteric message.

To understand the message one must be simple and live the message.

Simple messages reveal what Presence truly is – a conscious child.

It is the duty of a true school to disseminate the knowledge of the system as extensively as possible because men are in desperate need of these great ideas. They are the only ideas on earth that can relieve men from bondage, and the chains are stronger than iron. They can be sundered only by Self-remembering.

Being on the way means that one is part of the inner circle, which must transmit knowledge as objectively as possible.

The inner circle is a state. It is primarily based upon a high valuation for one's Self. Physical distance is not an impediment for a real student.

The task of our school is unlike any other task in recorded history.

Our school is designed by Influence C to form an ark and protect religion and the arts.

It is more important for our ark to conserve than to create.

It is our task to collect the message from all the schools that have preceded us.

We are not merely collecting esoteric messages but also focusing on being the message – making it our own.

The aim now is to leave as many conscious traces here as possible to enable those who follow to escape as well.

Mr. Gurdjieff suffered far beyond the understanding of men number four to acquire the knowledge for them. His task was to write it in clear and precise fashion. It is our task to be the words.

Schools are meant to produce multiple remarkable men – conscious beings – simultaneously. In schools multiple conscious beings can be produced at the same time with the same task.

In our school, it is a time for the conscious liberation of women. We are the carriers of the eternal flame of schools and our light shines brightly.

The aim of Influence C in creating a new civilization is to produce people they can reach.

We bring the vista of what we see to Apollo. We want to focus on European art and ideals. As the city signifies Presence, we want to leave Apollo beautiful and free of imagination.

We are closing the sequence of civilizations. The Old Kingdom opened it.

The ancient millennial conscious light has made a complete sweep of the sequence of civilizations and the deathless eternal gods. It begins anew with Apollo, which is on the same latitude as Athens.

Outside the celestial city of Paradise, our school and Apollo are the greatest opportunity to awaken, not just on earth, but in the entire universe.

CHAPTER 22

From Third Eye to Third Eye

The teaching passes from Third Eye to Third Eye – from Presence to Presence.

Although every second of our lives is equally important, the hour of the meetings is vital. Influence C are with us, directly instructing our Third Eye.

Angels create the keys, and angels reveal their inner meaning. The entire process flows directly from their Third Eye into our Third Eye.

The system is the most precious gift given to man because it presents an objective way to create an Astral Body; it nourishes our Soul and enables us to escape. One must treat it with greater care than one would an ancient wine.

Passing the torch of awakening is not merely ceremonial – it is a real process.

One has to teach to understand the system.

Anything Influence C help you learn is intended to help all students.

Teaching is very tricky. One has to do it with love or it is the lower self doing it. If one does not teach with love and essence Presence, it is ineffective.

I cannot sit up here and just impart information. I must be present and in love with each one of you young conscious beings, and you must be in the state of conscious love to receive this. That is what is occurring here.

I find that if I start talking about the knowledge of the system, it raises everyone's state, including my own.

The only way to speak with authority is to speak from conscious experience.

No teacher brings a new message; they just make the old one work.

A real teacher has to produce the states he talks about.

In sports, some instructors teach well, but do not play well. In the master game of awakening, one must both play well and teach well.

It is a law that when you escape, you must help someone else escape.

There are certain things one can learn only through teaching, and second line of work is designed so that students in the school have an opportunity to teach.

There is a special art to giving and receiving photographs well.

Be sure it is from the sincerity of essence and from the state of Presence.

Photographs should be presented and received as theories, not facts.

It is a mistake to think one can instruct only with words; one instructs with noble bearing, another with unswerving fidelity, another with frugality, another with charity, while yet another with modesty; and so it is with the other virtues.

Formatory mind thinks one must speak in order to instruct. Many students of Mr. Ouspensky were baffled late in this noble teacher's task when he stopped speaking and began to demonstrate in the last month of his life the great being of a complete man number seven. The greatest actions remain non-verbal.

Eventually, one teaches by becoming the words.

To teach now, for all of us, means to share Presence together.

Later many of you will have to work with younger people on all the things I have worked on with you. It requires infinite patience.

Young students remind us that we speak to tender Souls.

The most important thing is to do what is right for a student's work.

I take great pleasure in making things as simple and clear as possible.

When one is looking for a school, one is, in fact, looking for one's Self. A teacher is ineffective if the students fail to look for their own Third Eye.

The more simply we can present, the more truthful we become.

In the end, it is not only about oneself escaping, but about how many others one helped to escape. If one successfully shares one's being, one helps others escape.

Leonardo lit my light, and my light lights your own. Although I am very close to his vision, he was an artist and I am a philosopher. He has taught me all I know. His genius was more in functions and mine is more in Higher Centers.

I have left you with all the light and love that I possibly could. Never imagine there is any higher third line work than a student's love for his teacher or a teacher's love for his student.

Awakening and evolving is much worse, and much better, than I imagined it to be – the agony and the ecstasy. My students and our future civilization are the fruition of our work.

I want to use whatever time I have left to help you create a permanent tendency to evolve and escape.

Your Soul is my art form, my task, my masterpiece.

Your Presence is my book.

It is a much bigger gift than any of us know to be associated with the conscious aspects of the Ray of Creation and the Absolute. When I complete my role, never think of me as one who was with you, but rather as one who *is* with you.

If you knew what Influence C know, you would all stand up and dance.

The Thirty Great Work 'I's

1. Be	Be present.
2. Hold	Hold the sequence with presence.
3. Still	Control the moving center.
4. Back	Watch the lower self.
5. Turn	Return to the theme of the sequence, *e.g.*, *Look* or *Hear*.
6. Long *BE*	Prolong presence.
7. Act	Engage presence.
8. Peace (*Pax*)	Avoid the entire spectrum of negative emotions.
9. Leave	Avoid identification.
10. Kneel	Do not resent friction.
11. Drop	Do not judge or keep accounts.
12. Use	Use voluntary suffering.
13. Wit	Avoid wit.
14. Now	Think neither of the past nor of the future.
15. Look	Look with presence.
16. Hear	Hear with presence.

17. Feel	Feel with presence.
18. Taste	Taste with presence.
19. Smell	Smell with presence.
20. Move	Move with presence.
21. Talk	Speak with presence.
22. Think	Think with presence.
23. Read	Read with presence.
24. Write	Write with presence.
25. Child	Remain in essence; avoid false personality.
26. Serve	Do not inner consider, externally consider.
27. Scale	Use scale and relativity.
28. Aim	Keep aim and complete octaves; be aware of third forces.
29. Time	Remember the brevity of life.
30. Gods	Remember the gods.

The sequence uses one of the thirty great work 'I's for a theme, in the format:

*"Be, Hold, Theme, Back, Theme, **BE**." -- Four Wordless Breaths*

The Work 'I's most commonly used as a theme are: *Look, Hear, Feel*, and *Move*.

Glossary

This Glossary provides a brief description of terms used in this book. More complete explanations of these and other work terms are found in the works of Peter Ouspensky such as *In Search of the Miraculous* and *The Fourth Way*.

Absolute, the. The totality of everything that exists or could exist, more specifically, ultimate consciousness, the highest intelligence, or Supreme Being.

Acceptance. An esoteric tool, acceptance is a step towards the creation of higher states by seeing and working with things as they are.

Accounts, Keeping. Remembering real or imagined wrongs and allowing one's dealings with others to be affected by them.

Active Force. First force, that which starts a change or action. See also, Forces, Three.

Angels. The level of higher forces directly above mankind. See also, Influence C.

Apollo. The headquarters of the Fellowship of Friends, it consists of several structures and extensive grounds. All members in good standing may participate in the cultural and spiritual life of Apollo; they also contribute financially and through service to its construction and operations. Formerly called Renaissance and Mount Carmel.

Astral Body. A metaphysical body capable of existing independently of the physical body. See also, Higher Centers and Divine Presence.

Awakening. The process of Higher Centers beginning to function, gradually becoming more aware of the truth about oneself and reality; gaining an ever higher level of being.

Awakening, Relative. The condition of one who is less asleep, but who has not yet reached the level of a man number five or higher.

Being. (1) The accumulated effect of efforts to awaken – the ability to be the words, *i.e.*, to put the theories of the system into practice, not just to know them. (2) Accumulated experience in, as opposed to mere knowledge of, a particular area of endeavor, *e.g.,* in cooking, one who is able to do more than just follow a recipe has being in cooking.

Being, Level of. Degree of advancement in being. (1) Relative to Higher Centers, the degree to which one can control the lower self, reside in higher states, and live the ideas of the system. (2) Degree of experience in other areas of endeavor.

Being Present. The Third or Fourth State. See also, Divine

Presence.Beloved, the. An esoteric key derived from Sufism, the term "Beloved" refers to the Third or Fourth State of consciousness, that is, to Divine Presence or one's own Soul.

Body Types. An ancient system of classification of humans into seven types: Solar, Lunar, Venusian, Mercurial, Saturnine, Martial, and Jovial. Each type has particular physical and psychological traits, including a ruling endocrine gland. Relative to awakening, there is no advantage to being one type or another. See *The Theory of Celestial Influence* by Rodney Collin for a more complete explanation of body types.

Buffer. A psychological belief, attitude, or feature such as fear that prevents one from seeing or experiencing the reality of the present moment and one's true nature.

C Influence. Usually refers to higher forces. See also, Influence C.

Center(s). The seven centers of activity in a human. The four lower centers are: (1) the instinctive center, which governs routine bodily functions, *e.g.,* the five senses; (2) the moving center, which orients one in space and directs movement; (3) the emotional center, home of feelings and emotions; and (4) the intellectual center, *e.g.,* thought and reason. Fifth is the sex center. See, Sex Energy. Higher Centers are the remaining two centers. See, Higher Centers. The Introduction addresses centers and how they relate to the work.

Center of Gravity. Humans relate to the world primarily through one of the four lower centers, usually seeing their own center of gravity as more important or as a strength.

Conscience. Insight as a result of a higher state, as opposed to training or programming in the four lower centers as to what is right and wrong.

Conscious Being. A person who has achieved at least the level of being of a man number five. The term refers to such beings both before and after death.

Conscious Child. Essence aware of itself, Higher Centers functioning; it is the most real part of a person. It is from one's conscious child within that the Higher Self evolves.

Conscious Teaching. A teaching begun by a conscious being that assists those interested in evolving by developing their ability to experience higher states of consciousness; such a teaching has the assistance of higher forces.

Consciousness. One's state or degree of awakening or awareness.

Consciousness, Four States of. First state is what is commonly called sleep, *i.e.*, when one retires to bed for deep rest. Second state is characterized by movement which produces the illusion of reality and is therefore also called sleep. In second state one speaks, reads, writes, and so forth; it is the usual state of humans. The Third State is the Higher Emotional Center, sometimes called subjective consciousness; the Fourth State is the Higher Mental Center, sometimes called objective consciousness.

Crystallization. An event during which Higher Centers become permanent.

Denying Force. Second Force; that which opposes or resists First Force. See also, Forces, Three.

Divided Attention. An intentional effort to be aware of two or more things at once, one of them being oneself. Divided attention is Self-remembering, not multi-tasking.

Divine Presence. The Third or Fourth State in which Higher Centers are awake and attentive to what is in the moment. These states are associated with separation from imagination, identification, and negative emotions. See also, Higher Centers.

Effort. Using any of the techniques designed to promote higher states, such as school exercises, work 'I's, the sequence, or separating from friction.

Emotions, Negative. Negative feelings such as anger, jealousy, irritation, self-pity, and boredom. The system promotes the non-expression (not repression) and transformation of these emotions because the energy from them can be transformed into higher states, as opposed to being discharged or leaked out of the machine by various forms of expression.

Escaping. Awakening from mechanicality and the recurrence of many lives.

Essence. The qualities of an individual that are inherent at birth, including a core of awareness, plus physical and psychological traits. Essence usually develops only during the first few years of life; later it is largely obscured by false personality. Essence can be educated and developed further; the state of essence is the bridge to Higher Centers.

Evolve; Evolution. The child within (essence) becomes aware of itself and educates itself; through accumulating moments of Presence one's level of being grows.

Exercises. Intentionally planned efforts designed to promote Presence. For example, a listening exercise brings attention to sounds as a means of being present.

External Consideration. Thinking about others from the standpoint of what is good for their evolution. The opposite is inner considering, *i.e.,* concern about how others see you.

Fate. What is meant to be. If one has conscious fate, any significant action is monitored by higher forces; nevertheless, one must take responsibility for one's actions.

Features. Mechanical attitudes about oneself and one's relation to the world. The principal features are vanity, power, dominance, non-existence, greed, tramp, fear, naïveté, willfulness, and lunatic. Each person has one chief feature while others are secondary. Resisting features helps produce Higher Centers.

Fellowship of Friends, Inc. The esoteric school founded by Robert Burton in 1970. Its headquarters, called Apollo, is in northern California.

Feminine Dominance. Largely unseen attitudes about the way things "should be" that cause one to feel compelled to act in socially acceptable ways. Examples include feelings of obligation towards others and the compulsion to shame others into behaving better.

First Line of Work. Work for oneself. See also, Lines of Work.

First State. Ordinary sleep, usually in bed. See also, Consciousness, Four States of.

Forces, Higher. Any of the levels of intelligence and consciousness above man. Synonym for Influence C, and beings such as gods or angels.

Forces, Three. The three elements or energies which must be present before any real change or action can occur. The three forces are: First, *Active Force*: the element which initiates a change or action; Second, *Passive,* or *Denying Force*: that which opposes, resists, or is material for the first force; and, Third, *Neutralizing Force:* the force that allows the tension between the First and Second Forces to be resolved.

Formatory Mind. Automatic, unthinking responses according to fixed patterns or ideas; the activity of the mechanical part of the intellectual center. It often includes opposite thinking, unexamined attitudes and beliefs, and erroneous "facts".

Four Wordless Breaths. Being present and silent for the space of four breaths. A higher state. See also, Divine Presence and Sequence, the.

Friction. In general, troubles of any kind that are experienced as problems. Also, the internal struggle between the part of one that wants to awaken and anything that interferes with that aim. Friction is subjective and much depends on one's attitudes towards events.

Functions. The four lower centers which operate mechanically, with or without attention. Highly developed functions, such as being an exceptional musician, athlete, or scholar, should not be mistaken for a higher level of consciousness.

God. Generally refers to "the God within," that is, one's Higher Centers. See also, Absolute, the, which refers to the Supreme Being.

Gods. Angels or Influence C. See also, Influence C.

Good Householder. A person who values things appropriately and tries to take care of his/her body, possessions, environment, and relationships with others. Work on consciousness can begin once one reaches the level of good householder.

Gurdjieff, George. An Armenian Greek born in the late nineteenth century, Gurdjieff traveled extensively throughout the Middle East and Asia to collect the esoteric knowledge that forms the basis of the system. He left Russia following the 1917 Revolution and eventually settled in Paris, where he taught until his death in 1949.

Higher Centers. Higher Emotional Center (Third State or World 12) and Higher Mental Center (Fourth State or World 6). Higher Emotional, which perceives the connectedness of all things, is the seat of conscious love and compassion. Higher Mental, which perceives the laws that govern all things, is the seat of conscious wisdom. Higher Centers are known by many names, including: Real 'I,' Third Eye, Higher Self, Soul, Self, Divine Presence, and Four Wordless Breaths.

Higher Forces. Metaphysical beings above the level of humans, they are also called gods, angels, and Influence C. See also, Influence C.

Higher Self. Essence transcends into Higher Self when Higher Centers are functioning. See also, Higher Centers and Lower Self (that which opposes the Higher Self).

Higher States. The states associated with the functioning of Higher Centers, *i.e.,* the third and fourth states of consciousness.

Horn, Alex. Robert Earl Burton's esoteric teacher from 1967 to 1969.

'I'. Usually refers to one of the many 'I's. Lacking unity, consciousness, and will, they are distinguished from Higher Centers, which are Real 'I'.

Identification. (1) The state in which one's attention is focused on something to the exclusion of everything else; the opposite of separation. (2) The tendency, especially of false personality, to place one's sense of identity in things that are external. All identification, even with the system, is contrary to the functioning of Higher Centers.

Imagination. The state in which a person's attention is devoted to things that are not actually in the moment. Also, the false picture one has of oneself and one's abilities.

Impressions. Perceptions that are received through the senses, they are a form of food for the body and for Higher Centers. An impression may be good, bad, or indifferent.

Influence A and B. Influences A are those that concern the basic needs of the machine, *e.g.,* food, shelter, security, and ego. B influence originated as C Influence, but descended over time. It includes religions, healing arts, and martial arts; each of these may point towards the possibility of a higher mode of existence, but they ceased being C Influence when they lost direct connection to a conscious source.

Influence C. (1) Direct connection to the influence of a conscious being or his/her circle of influence. (2) Higher forces, also called gods or angels.

Inner Circle. People in a school of awakening who share a higher level of being and understanding and who are working towards a common aim. It is a state, not a place.

Inner Considering. Identification with one's lower self, especially how others view you.

Interval. When internal or external work seems to have paused, changed direction, or stopped. See also, Octave.

Keys. Symbols designed to evoke or instruct the Higher Self. Keys may be words, *e.g.,* veil, indicating imagination, or they may be visual, *e.g.,* a cube or square in a sculpture, signifying a higher state of consciousness.

King of Clubs. The intellectual part of the instinctive center. The brain behind the machine, it can shift energy to parts of the body that need it, as in fight-or-flight situations, or when ill. It can be intensely aware of its environment in a protective or predatory sense. In contrast, the increased awareness of higher states is softer and less concerned with the physical machine and its desires or fears. The king of clubs is very powerful, it can imitate consciousness, and it is the seat of the lower self.

King of Hearts. The intellectual part of the emotional center; it is the gateway to Higher Centers because it can be trained to experience life in ways approaching the experience of Higher Centers. As "steward," the king of hearts can act on what is learned in a higher state, control the other parts of the machine, and employ techniques such as the sequence or work 'I's with the intent of evoking Higher Centers.

Kings. The intellectual part of each of the four lower centers. See also, Centers.

Law of Accident. The influence of random forces or accident on a person, in contrast to influences such as cause-and-effect, fate, and conscious will.

Life. Human activity not associated with a school of awakening.

Light, Created and Uncreated. Created light is a higher state resulting from one's efforts using the sequence or other work tools. Uncreated light is a higher state that arrives in various other ways such as by being with others who are in a state of Presence.

Lines of Work. The three lines are: first, work for oneself; second, work for and with others; and, third, work for the Teacher or the school. An interval in one of the lines may be bridged by activity in one or both of the other two. See also, Octave.

Long *BE*. The sixth (last) step of the sequence, as distinguished from the first step, "short *Be*." See also, Sequence, the.

Lower Self. The four lower centers functioning unconsciously, *i.e.,* animal intelligence in human form; the most mechanical aspect of a person. See also, King of Clubs.

Machine, the. The physical body from the point of view that all its activity tends to occur automatically and mechanically in response to stimuli.

Magnetic Center. The part of one's personality (a group of 'I's) that is attracted to Influence B and that may eventually lead one to seek a school and Influence C.

Man Number One, Two, and Three. A person (male or female) whose center of gravity is in one of the four lower centers. Number one is a moving or instinctive type; number two is emotionally centered; number three is intellectually centered.

Man Number Four. A product of school work; a student of the system (male or female) who tries to apply work ideas; one who has a center of gravity in the work.

Man Number Five. A person in whom the Higher Emotional Center has begun to function more regularly. He or she is said to have subjective consciousness.

Man Number Six. A person in whom Higher Centers have crystallized, *i.e.,* become permanent. At this level one is said to have objective consciousness; Higher Centers can be evoked at will. The eternal flame is ignited, but wanes.

Man Number Seven. A person who has achieved all that is possible, in terms of higher consciousness, for a human being on earth.

Many 'I's. All of the thoughts, emotions, sensations, etc. originating in the four lower centers and the sex center. The many 'I's lack unity, will, and consciousness, which are properties of Real 'I'. The many 'I's are the restless mind, *i.e.,* "the ten thousand."

Mechanical Goodness. Being good with no particular aim or attention; acting from others' expectations about what should be done in a situation or to avoid criticism.

Mechanicality. Acting like a stimulus-response machine, that is, without conscious direction. It generally refers to having only automatic responses to stimuli.

Message, the. Schools produce messages designed to awaken Third Eye. Presence is the heart of the message. When it receives school messages, Third Eye knows itself and rises into being.

Microcosmos. A human considered as a miniature cosmos, that is, as a replica of the fundamental patterns of the universe.

Negativity. Any negative expression in one of the four lower centers, especially when accompanied by a negative emotion. Examples of negativity include unhappy or disapproving verbal or facial expressions as well as threatening postures or movements.

Nine of Hearts. The emotional part of the king of hearts. See also, Queen, White.

Octave. Refers to the Law of Octaves, which describes how events proceed through steps (as in music) with intervals at mi-fa and si-do. Octaves are either ascending or descending. Intervals are the points at which the direction of an octave may change.

Ouspensky, Peter. A Russian mathematician, journalist, author, and student of George Gurdjieff. Ouspensky established himself in London, where he taught until his death in 1947. His books, including *In Search of the Miraculous*, *The Fourth Way*, and *The Psychology of Man's Possible Evolution*, are good introductions to the system.

Passions. The many 'I's with all their desires and fears, and features. The steward must put the passions in order, *i.e.*, control the lower self in order to experience Presence.

Personality. (1) False personality is one's imaginary picture of oneself; developed in childhood, it includes acquired acts, attitudes, and rote responses that are used to protect essence. See also, Lower Self. (2) True personality is based on applying the system; it involves understanding one's essence and is intentionally developed to protect essence. More real than false personality, it works to attain and support higher consciousness.

Photograph. (1) (noun) An observation about the state or behavior of oneself or another; (2) (verb) Pointing out something in the moment, such as an instance of sleep or a shock.

Play, the. Events seen from the point of view that they occur under the guidance and control of higher forces, who are the authors of the play.

Presence. See, Divine Presence.

Queen, Black. The nine of clubs, *i.e.*, the emotional part of the king of clubs (not the Queen of Clubs); it is the part that opposes Presence and wants the machine to prevail.

Queen, White. The nine of hearts, *i.e.*, the emotional part of the king of hearts (not the queen of hearts). This part, which can bring work 'I's or the sequence to invoke Presence, is the most powerful part of the four lower centers and supports Presence when it occurs.

Ray of Creation. The levels of everything that exists. At the top is the Absolute (World 1); at the bottom is the moon (World 96). Each step down is more complex and subject to more laws. See also, Worlds.

Real 'I'. See, Higher Centers.

Relativity. Considering something, such as an event or another person, from different points of view. When one is identified all awareness is trapped in a single point of view.

Scale. Viewing an event or experience from the appropriate (large to small) perspective.

School. Refers to a school of awakening connected to higher forces. The thread or "vine" of schools has been virtually unbroken since prehistoric times. The term higher school refers to higher forces assisting schools on earth.

Second Line of Work. Work for and with others. See also, Lines of Work

Second State. See, Consciousness, Four States of, also Sleep.

Self-remembering. (1) A higher state of consciousness; see also, Higher Centers and Consciousness, Four States of. (2) The title of a book by Robert Earl Burton.

Separation. Maintaining a sense of self apart from one's sufferings and identifications. It is the aspect of Self-remembering that tries to see things objectively.

Sequence, the. The sequence is designed to help the Self remember itself. It uses one of the thirty work 'I's for a theme, in the format *Be, Hold, (Theme), Back, (Theme), BE,* intoned internally at a careful pace. The most commonly used themes are: *Look, Hear, Feel,* and *Move.* While one should be present at each step of the sequence, after the final *BE,* there should occur the four wordless breaths, *i.e.,* Presence without words.

Sex Energy. The energy of the sex center. It may be used for procreation, creating art, and/or to fuel Higher Centers, essence, and true personality. Used incorrectly, it can devolve into negative emotions, imagination, and identification.

Shocks. Unexpected events that interrupt second state sleep and help awaken us.

Short *Be*. The first word (*Be*) in a sequence; compare capitalization of long *BE*.

Sleep. In the system the second state of consciousness is often called sleep. See also, Consciousness, Four States of.

Soul. See, Higher Centers and Divine Presence.

State. See, Consciousness, Four States of.

Steward. A group of 'I's in the king of hearts that are able to observe oneself and to control the passions to some degree so as to assist in awakening Higher Centers.

Suffering, Transformation of. Accepting and separating from real or necessary suffering without negativity. Transformation involves the activity of Higher Centers and the king of hearts; it can lead to powerful experiences of increased consciousness.

Suffering, Unnecessary. Suffering that could be avoided by more intelligent attitudes and/or behaviors; it is a result of imagination or identification.

Suffering, Voluntary. Creating relatively minor discomfort or inconvenience for oneself in order to interrupt one's usual state and remind one to be present, *e.g.,* keeping one's feet flat on the floor while dining.

System, the. The theories and methods that may be used to awaken Higher Centers, evoke higher states, and become one's Higher Self. The system is esoteric knowledge passed on since prehistoric times and across many cultural traditions.

Tarot Card XXI. Implies triumphant success or fulfillment in reaching a higher state of consciousness. Usually shown as a young woman balanced on one foot.

Ten Thousand, the. The many 'I's. See also, Self, Lower.

Third Eye. A visual symbol, it often appears as an eye, a jewel, or special mark in the center of the forehead. Synonym for Higher Centers or awakened consciousness.

Third Line of Work. Work for the Teacher or the School. See also, Lines of Work

Third State. Higher Emotional Center. See also, Consciousness, Four States of.

Thirty Great Work 'I's. The Appendix contains a list of the thirty great work 'I's. They can be used in the sequence or individually for the purpose of creating Presence.

Tramp. A feature characterized by an inability to value things appropriately, tramp finds it difficult to take care of things, to take responsibility, and to pay one's fair share.

Unity. A state wherein the many 'I's are under the control of Higher Centers, *i.e.,* Real 'I'.

Veil. Imagination; all that stands between a person and a higher state.

Verify. To see for oneself the truth or validity of an idea of the system through personal experience. The emphasis is on practical application as opposed to theory.

Way, on the. A stage of development in which one has a permanent tendency to evolve that can pass from one lifetime to another. It implies a readiness to be responsible for one's own work and that of others.

Will. A state associated with the ability "to do," the ability to be one's own Real 'I'.

Work, the. Employing the system in a practical way; trying to be the words.

Work 'I'. Any word or thought that assists one to make efforts in furtherance of an aim to awaken. See the Appendix for a list of the thirty great work 'I's.

World 6. Higher Mental Center. See also, Higher Centers.

World 12. Higher Emotional Center. See also, Higher Centers.

Worlds 96, 48, 24, 12, 6, 3 and 1. Different levels of the Ray of Creation. World 96 corresponds to the level of false personality; World 48, true personality; World 24, essence; World 12, Higher Emotional; World 6, Higher Mental; Worlds 3 and 1 are the Absolute's Higher Emotional and Higher Mental respectively. See also, Ray of Creation.

The Fellowship of Friends

The Fellowship of Friends was founded in 1970 by Robert Earl Burton in the tradition of Fourth Way schools; it draws largely, but not exclusively, from the teachings of George Gurdjieff and Peter Ouspensky. The Fellowship's main location is at Apollo, a community in the foothills of California's Sierra Nevada mountains. Teaching Centers are maintained in major cities throughout the world, some of which are listed below:

Ahmedabad	Milan
Amsterdam	Moscow
Athens	New York
Beirut	Palo Alto
Berlin	Paris
Brussels	Rome
Buenos Aires	Sacramento
Copenhagen	San Francisco
Edinburgh	Sao Palo
Frankfurt	St. Petersburg
Istanbul	Taipei
Kiev	Tel Aviv
London	Tijuana
Los Ángeles	Tokyo
Madrid	Toronto
Mexico City	Washington, D.C.
Miami	Zurich

For more information on the Fellowship, details of membership, or to contact the center nearest you, please call or write the Fellowship of Friends:

Fellowship of Friends
P.O. Box 1000
Oregon House, CA 95962

Telephone: +1 (530) 300-5322

Robert Earl Burton is a spiritual master who has taught thousands of people since he founded the Fellowship of Friends in 1970. He initially relied largely on the esoteric system of awakening transmitted by Gurdjieff and Ouspensky. As Mr. Burton's personal work and ideas developed, he began to uncover the great truths and spiritual practices common to every system of awakening, from the prehistoric to the modern, from ancient Greek philosophy to world religions, and from obscure traditions as well. Over time he incorporated these ancient truths, images, and practices into his teaching, forging them into a practical school in which students learn to live the ideas, rather than merely know them intellectually.

Left: Mr. Burton teaching (2010)
Right: Statuette of a Phoenician goddess
(8th cent. BC), bronze & silver, Louvre

Printed in Great Britain
by Amazon

53241412R00112